3rd Shared Task on Discourse Relation Parsing and Treebanking (DISRPT 2023)

Toronto, Canada
14 July 2023

ISBN: 978-1-7138-8181-0

Printed from e-media with permission by:

Curran Associates, Inc.
57 Morehouse Lane
Red Hook, NY 12571

Some format issues inherent in the e-media version may also appear in this print version.

Printed with permission by Curran Associates, Inc. (2024)

Association for Computational Linguistics
209 N. Eighth Street
Stroudsburg, Pennsylvania 18360

Phone: 1-570-476-8006
Fax: 1-570-476-0860

acl@aclweb.org

Additional copies of this publication are available from:

Curran Associates, Inc.
57 Morehouse Lane
Red Hook, NY 12571 USA
Phone: 845-758-0400
Fax: 845-758-2633
Email: curran@proceedings.com
Web: www.proceedings.com

ACL-CODI 2023

The Shared Task on Discourse Relation Parsing and Treebanking

Proceedings of the 3rd Shared Task on Discourse Relation Parsing and Treebanking (DISRPT 2023)

July 14, 2023

Order copies of this and other ACL proceedings from:

Association for Computational Linguistics (ACL)
209 N. Eighth Street
Stroudsburg, PA 18360
USA
Tel: +1-570-476-8006
Fax: +1-570-476-0860
acl@aclweb.org

Preface

Welcome to the 3rd Shared Task on Discourse Relation Parsing and Treebanking (DISRPT 2023).

DISRPT is a shared task on discourse processing across formalisms, for a variety of languages and genres, with three subtasks this year: Task 1: discourse segmentation, Task 2: connective detection, and Task 3: relation classification.

We provided training, development, and test datasets from all available languages in RST, SDRT, PDTB and DEP (discourse dependencies), using a uniform format. Because different corpora, languages, and frameworks use different guidelines, the shared task aims at promoting the design of flexible methods for dealing with various guidelines, to propose a joint evaluation of discourse parsing approaches and to push forward the discussion on converging standards for discourse units and relations.

DISRPT 2023 is part of the CODI 2023 workshop, a venue that brings together researchers working on all aspects of discourse in Computational Linguistics and NLP. We hope that the next CODI workshops will also feature shared tasks on discourse analysis, as the domain needs more research promoting thorough and diversified evaluation as well as more consistent standards and expansions to languages and text types not yet covered in the field.

We thank the CODI organizers, and the reviewers who helped improve the papers and reproduce the participating systems. Finally we would like to thank the ACL 2023 workshop chairs Eduardo Blanco, Yang Feng, and Annie Louis who organized the ACL workshops program.

The DISRPT 2023 Organizers,

Chloé Braud, Yang Janet Liu, Eleni Metheniti, Philippe Muller, Laura Rivière, Attapol Te Rutherford and Amir Zeldes

Program Committee

Chairs

Chloé Braud, IRIT, CNRS
Yang Janet Liu, Georgetown University
Eleni Metheniti, IRIT, University of Toulouse
Philippe Muller, IRIT, University of Toulouse
Laura Rivière, IRIT
Attapol Rutherford, Chulalongkorn University
Amir Zeldes, Georgetown University

Program Committee

Chloé Braud, IRIT, CNRS
Yang Janet Liu, Georgetown University
Eleni Metheniti, IRIT, University of Toulouse
Philippe Muller, IRIT, University of Toulouse
Laura Rivière, IRIT
Amir Zeldes, Georgetown University

Table of Contents

Program

Friday, July 14, 2023

11:00 - 11:15 *Opening Remarks*

The DISRPT 2023 Shared Task on Elementary Discourse Unit Segmentation, Connective Detection, and Relation Classification
Chloé Braud, Yang Janet Liu, Eleni Metheniti, Philippe Muller, Laura Rivière, Attapol Rutherford and Amir Zeldes

11:15 - 12:15 *Shared Task papers*

DiscoFlan: Instruction Fine-tuning and Refined Text Generation for Discourse Relation Label Classification
Kaveri Anuranjana

DisCut and DiscReT: MELODI at DISRPT 2023
Eleni Metheniti, Chloé Braud, Philippe Muller and Laura Rivière

HITS at DISRPT 2023: Discourse Segmentation, Connective Detection, and Relation Classification
Wei Liu, Yi Fan and Michael Strube

12:15 - 12:30 *Discussion of future shared tasks*

The DISRPT 2023 Shared Task on Elementary Discourse Unit Segmentation, Connective Detection, and Relation Classification *

[1,2,3]**Chloé Braud** and [4]**Yang Janet Liu** and [1]**Eleni Metheniti** and [1,3]**Philippe Muller**

[1]**Laura Rivière** and [5]**Attapol T. Rutherford** and [4]**Amir Zeldes**
[1]UT3 - IRIT ; [2]CNRS ; [3]ANITI ; [4]Georgetown University
[1]firstname.lastname@irit.fr [5]attapol.t@chula.ac.th
[4]{yl879,amir.zeldes}@georgetown.edu

Abstract

In 2023, the third iteration of the DISRPT Shared Task (**Dis**course **R**elation **P**arsing and **T**reebanking) was held, dedicated to the underlying units used in discourse parsing across formalisms. Following the success of the 2019 and 2021 tasks on Elementary Discourse Unit Segmentation, Connective Detection, and Relation Classification, this iteration has added 10 new corpora, including 2 new languages (Thai and Italian) and 3 discourse treebanks annotated in the discourse dependency representation in addition to the previously included frameworks: RST, SDRT, and PDTB. In this paper, we review the data included in DISRPT 2023, which covers 26 datasets across 13 languages, survey and compare submitted systems, and report on system performance on each task for both treebanked and plain-tokenized versions of the data.

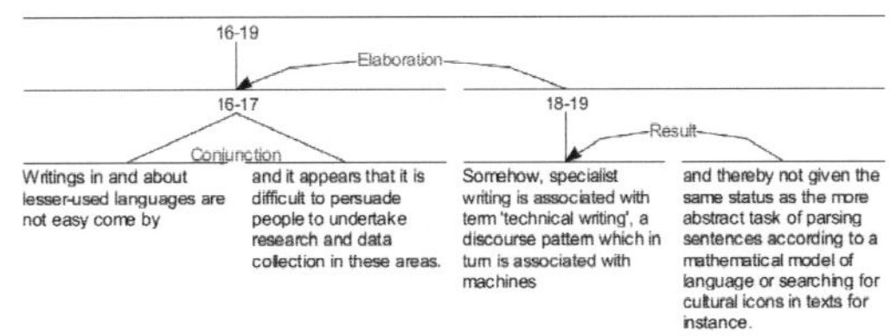

Figure 1: An RST Tree Example (Iruskieta et al., 2015).

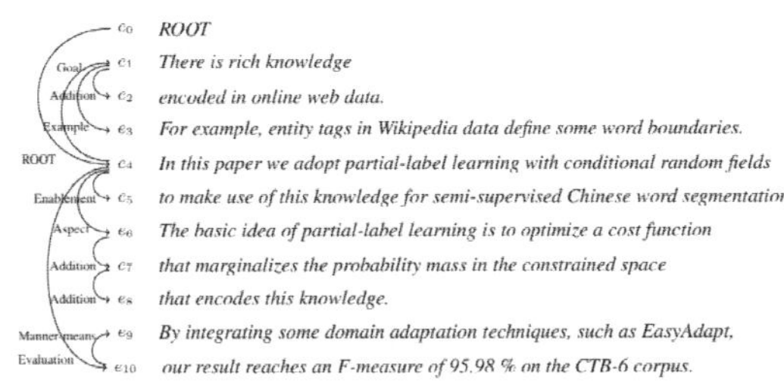

Figure 2: A Dependency Example (Yang and Li, 2018).

1 Introduction

Discourse parsing aims to uncover the underlying structure of monologues or dialogues, where spans of texts are linked together by semantic-pragmatic discourse relations such as EXPLANATION, CONTRAST, TEMPORAL-ASYNCHRONOUS, or GOAL. Examples of such structures in different representations are given in Figures 1 and 2. Several theoretical frameworks have been proposed for discourse analysis and have subsequently been used in many annotation projects. Common ones include the Rhetorical Structure Theory (RST, Mann and Thompson 1988), where discourse structures are hierarchical constituent trees (Figure 1), and relation definitions are based on authors' or speakers' intents; the Segmented Discourse Representation Theory (SDRT, Asher and Lascarides 2003), where structures are graphs with non-terminal nodes, and relations are defined using formal logics; and the Penn Discourse Treebank (PDTB, Prasad et al. 2005) with relations between isolated pairs of argument spans, possibly marked by a connective (e.g. *but*, *because*) which is then annotated a sense label. In addition, building upon several studies proposing to encode discourse structures as dependencies (Hirao et al., 2013; Muller et al., 2012), it has been proposed to annotate discourse graphs using pure dependency structures, with no non-terminal nodes (Figure 2), while keeping relations and segmentation rules from RST—which is abbreviated here as the DEP framework (Yang and Li, 2018).

Within each framework, numerous corpora of a variety of languages and domains have been annotated. However, the differences between the annotation projects hinder the evaluation of the progress made and to develop systems that should ideally perform well on the broadest possible range of data. Zeldes et al. (2019) proposed the first iteration of the shared task of Discourse Relation Parsing and

*Discourse Relation Parsing and Treebanking (DISRPT 2023) was held in conjunction with CODI at ACL 2023 in Toronto, Canada and Online (https://sites.google.com/view/disrpt2023/).

Proceedings of the 3rd Shared Task on Discourse Relation Parsing and Treebanking (DISRPT 2023), pages 1–21
July 14, 2023 ©2023 Association for Computational Linguistics

Treebanking (DISRPT)[1] in order to broaden the scope of discourse studies by including datasets and inviting researchers from different discourse theories, to facilitate cross-framework studies.

The first edition of the DISRPT shared task was limited to **Task 1: discourse segmentation**—identifying the elementary discourse units (EDUs) that may be linked by discourse relations; and **Task 2: discourse connective detection**—identifying specific lexical items, called connectives, that can signal a discourse relation (e.g. *while, because, since, as long as* etc.). In 2021, for the second edition, Zeldes et al. (2021) added a third task, **Task 3: discourse relation classification**—identifying a relation label between a pair of attached discourse units.[2] This year, for the third edition, we maintained the three tasks but expanded the benchmark with 10 new corpora, including datasets from the DEP framework: in total, 26 corpora were made available across 4 frameworks and 13 languages in a unified format. In the last phase of the shared task, we released 6 surprise datasets including data for a new language (Thai), as well as 4 out-of-domain (OOD) corpora for which only dev and test partitions were available.

Three teams participated in the shared task, with one team including half of the organizers of the shared task. Overall, two systems were proposed for Tasks 1 and 2, and three systems for Task 3. Two systems are based on fine-tuning Transformer masked language model encoders, while the third one relies on a generative transformer model for relation classification. Only one team presented results for all tasks and tracks (MELODI), and another team (HITS) reported results for all tasks but were limited to the Treebanked track (i.e. parsed and gold sentence-split data) for Tasks 1 and 2. The third team (DiscoFLAN) focused on relation classification only. For the Treebanked track, MELODI ranked first on the EDU segmentation task, and HITS ranked first on the connective detection task with very similar mean scores. For relation classification, HITS ranked first.

2 Related Work

Automatic discourse analysis is an active domain of research, with increasing interests for the past few years as tools become increasingly capable of handling such tasks, and discourse information can be helpful for many applications, for example for authorship attribution (Ferracane et al., 2017; Feng, 2015), fake news or political bias detection (Karimi and Tang, 2019; Devatine et al., 2022), sentiment analysis (Bhatia et al., 2015; Huber and Carenini, 2020), or for generation, with uses in machine translation (Tu et al., 2013; Joty et al., 2017; Webber et al., 2013) or summarization (Louis et al., 2010; Hirao et al., 2013; Yoshida et al., 2014; Liu et al., 2019; Chen and Yang, 2021; Hewett and Stede, 2022; Pu et al., 2023).

Discourse parsing is the full task of recovering a discourse structure of a document, either constituent trees in the RST-based framework, dependency trees for DEP, or graphs for SDRT. Performance is still far from perfect for full discourse parsing, and systems are mostly developed for English, monologues, and the newswire domain, using the largest news corpus available, the RST-DT (Carlson et al., 2001), with an F1 score of 55.4 at best for full trees (Kobayashi et al., 2022).

Recent studies also sometimes report results on other datasets, especially on GUM (e.g. Atwell et al. 2022; Yu et al. 2022b), the largest RST English corpus to date, which is composed of multiple spoken and written genres (Zeldes, 2017). Very recently, Liu and Zeldes (2023) showed the lack of generalization of existing SOTA RST discourse parsers through a series of experiments, with a significant performance drop when applied to unseen genres, and also demonstrated the importance of heterogeneous training data for robust discourse parsing.

A few attempts have also been made to develop systems for dialogues, especially using the SDRT STAC corpus (Asher et al., 2016) with either supervised methods (Liu and Chen, 2021; Chi and Rudnicky, 2022; Yu et al., 2022a) or transfer learning strategies given the small size of the dataset (e.g. Fan et al. 2022).

Finally, multilingual RST discourse parsing has been the topic of a few work (Braud et al., 2017a; Liu et al., 2020, 2021) involving transfer to tackle data scarcity. Liu et al. (2021) in particular demonstrated that cross-lingual strategies could even help for English, and also that good segmentation is crucial for full discourse parsing, with a loss of up to 8% when using predicted EDUs.

As a matter of fact, an option to better understand the difficulty and low performance of discourse parsing is to examine its constituent subtasks, such

[1] https://sites.google.com/view/disrpt2019

[2] https://sites.google.com/georgetown.edu/disrpt2021

as discourse segmentation, but also relation classification, and attachment ('naked' or unlabeled tree building). Many studies have been dedicated to these subtasks, with a specific focus on the first two. The aim of the DISRPT shared task is precisely to provide benchmarks for these critical steps toward full discourse parsing, to the extent possible in a formalism-neutral way, allowing participants to demonstrate the generalizability of their systems across languages, domains, and frameworks.

Discourse segmentation in particular has been seen as a solved task with performance as high as 94% on RST-DT as early as over 10 years ago (Xuan Bach et al., 2012). However, systems at the time were trained only on English newswires data with gold information about sentence boundaries and morpho-syntactic features. When facing realistic data in other languages and even in English, with systems based on predicted information, performance drops very substantially (Braud et al., 2017b). Disparities across languages and datasets were later emphasized within the DISRPT shared tasks (Zeldes et al., 2019, 2021) under realistic settings (with predicted sentence splits), with performance above 95% for some corpora, but scores in the 80s for the Spanish SCTB (82.5% at best), the Chinese SCTB (83.3), or the Russian RRT (86.2%). The best-performing system in 2019 (Muller et al., 2019) used a single multilingual BERT (Devlin et al., 2019) based model for every corpus, while in the second edition of DISRPT (Zeldes et al., 2021), the winning system (Gessler et al., 2021) achieved the best performance with an accuracy of around 91.5% on average, which relied on varied language models, either mono- or multilingual, as well as hand-crafted features. A loss of about 2% was observed when gold sentence boundaries are not given.

For Task 3, discourse relation classification is often further decomposed into different types of relations: **explicit relations**—ones that are triggered by a discourse connective (e.g. *while, because*), and **implicit relations** —ones that do not contain a discourse marker. The latter is considered a harder task, since no explicit cues are present, and has thus been studied more extensively (e.g. Kim et al. 2020; Liang et al. 2020; Long and Webber 2022).

For explicit relations, the task generally reduces to identifying the connectives, that is deciding whether a token such as 'and' is being used as a discourse marker, and then identifying the relation, with the connective constraining the possible labels (e.g. 'and' can signal EXPANSION or RESULT, but not PURPOSE). Connective detection and explicit discourse relation classification have been considered easy tasks, with high performance (Pitler et al., 2008), but it was later shown that performance drops drastically on non-news domains, or in languages with small datasets (Xue et al., 2016; Scholman et al., 2021; Johannsen and Søgaard, 2013).

For the first two editions of DISRPT, rather high performance was reported for connective detection: between an F1 score of 92-94 for the English and Turkish corpora, and an F1 score of 87 for the Chinese one, with only a small drop when gold sentence splits are not provided. However, this may be due to the relatively large and homogeneous datasets used in the evaluation. This year's new edition introduces 6 new corpora for Task 2, as well as OOD datasets for which no training data is available: this has made the task more challenging, with the mean scores now under 80% (see Section 5 below for details). We also report scores for implicit vs explicit relation classification for some corpora, which were not available in DISRPT 2021, and demonstrate low scores for implicit relations as well when data is scarce.

The DISRPT Shared Task is among the very few studies to report scores for both implicit and explicit (also including other types such as AltLex markers, see Prasad et al. 2014) relation classification, thus making it more practical for models to be able to recognize any types of relations. Task 3 was introduced in 2021, and the winning system was Transformers-based language-specific models for each target language and a set of hand-crafted features: overall the average performance was nevertheless still rather low (61.8%), showing room for substantial improvement.

3 Tasks and Tracks

Three tasks were proposed for DISRPT 2023:

[1] **Discourse Unit Segmentation**—the task consists of identifying each token as the start of an EDU or not (BO scheme at the token level).

[2] **Discourse Connective Detection**—the task consists of identifying each token as starting, being inside, or outside a discourse connective (i.e. BIO scheme at the token level).

[3] **Discourse Relation Classification**—the task

consists of assigning a label to a pair of textual segments, given that a relation holds between the two units (i.e. multi-class classification).

While all corpora have data annotated for Task 3, note that they are not all relevant for Tasks 1 and 2:

- For corpora within the PDTB framework: the connectives are annotated, but no discourse segments are identified (i.e. Task 2 but not Task 1).
- Corpora within RST, SDRT, and DEP: the EDUs are identified, but not connectives (Task 1 but not Task 2).

The shared task also proposes two tracks for Tasks 1 and 2:

- **Treebanked**: data is tokenized, split into sentences, and parsed (morpho-syntactic information is given). When gold information was available in the original corpus, it is provided as is. Otherwise, we provided predicted annotations done with Stanza (Qi et al., 2020).
- **Plain**: data is tokenized and split into documents.

4 Shared Task Data

4.1 DISRPT Format

The goal of the Shared Task is to provide a unified format across corpora annotated in different frameworks.

Data Format Three types of formats are provided for each partition (train / dev / test) of each corpus. The `.conllu` and `.tok` files are the data for Tasks 1 and 2, and they correspond to the Treebanked and Plain tracks respectively. Meta-information is provided for documents in both formats. The `.conllu` files also have sentence annotation,[3] part-of-speech (POS), and syntactic parse information, obtained either from Stanza or from gold standard treebanking. Some corpora have multi-word annotations: that is, both the contracted forms (indicated with specific IDs such as '`2-3 can't`') and the sub-forms ('`2 can`' and '`3 not`') appear in the files. Segmentation is indicated with a single label at the beginning of an EDU, at the position of the first token. The connective labels correspond to 2 labels: one indicating the beginning ('B') of a connective, and the other for tokens inside ('I') a connective. Note that discontinuous connectives (e.g. 'either ... or') are annotated as separate single connectives.[4]

The `.rels` files are for Task 3: each line corresponds to a pair of attached discourse units, with the annotation of the original relation from the corpus, and the label used for the shared task: in particular, PDTB-style relations are truncated at level 2 (e.g. CONTINGENCY.CAUSE.RESULT > CONTINGENCY.CAUSE, and RST-DT relations are grouped into 17 classes as done in Carlson and Marcu (2001). In addition, for the 2023 edition, some mappings were performed in order to make the data more homogeneous: only minimal modifications were done including correcting misspelling and non-significant merging such as E-ELAB > E-ELABORATION, SOLUTION-HOOD > SOLUTION-HOOD, and TOPICOMMENT > TOPIC-COMMENT. The full mapping is given in Table 7 in Appendix A. The files also contain sentence contexts for each span, indicate discontinuities in the spans, and provide the direction of the relation (unit 1 to unit 2: `1>2`; or the reverse `1<2`).

Changes since DISRPT 2021 The major change is the newly added 10 corpora, including datasets without training data with the aim of better testing models' generalizability. In addition to the minimal relations mappings described above, we also add the annotation of multi-word expressions in more corpora, for consistency.

4.2 Summary of the Datasets

In total, this year's DISRPT shared task included 26 corpora annotated across 4 frameworks and 13 languages. We provide general statistics of each dataset in Table 8 in Appendix B. For more information, please consult the relevant publications provided in the last column of the table.

The corpora vary not only in terms of languages and sizes, but also their genres and domains, including news, wiki, scientific documents, conversations, and so on. Corpora vary tremendously in extent: as shown in the upper part of Table 8 (RST, SDRT and DEP frameworks), the largest corpora contain more than 300 documents and 200k tokens, while

[3] For the ita.pdtb.luna, containing dialogue transcription, we rather use an 'utterance' unit that corresponds to a sequence of speech between two silences.

[4] We found that the annotation was faulty in the Thai corpus, where discontinuous connectives were annotated as one single chain of 'B/I' labels, thus allowing 'I' labels to appear with no immediately preceding 'B'. This annotation will be corrected in the GitHub repository (`https://github.com/disrpt/sharedtask2023/`) for future use, and we will indicate the possible impact on the scores.

Corpus	Train					Dev					Test				
	#Docs	#EDUs	#Conn	#Labels	#Rels	#Docs	#EDUs	#Conn	#Labels	#Rels	#Docs	#EDUs	#Conn	#Labels	#Rels
Tasks 1 and 3: Segmentation and Relations															
deu.rst.pcc	142	2449	-	26	2164	17	275	-	24	241	17	294	-	24	260
***eng.dep.covdtb**	-	-	-	-	-	150	2754	-	12	2399	150	2951	-	12	2586
eng.dep.scidtb	492	6740	-	24	6060	154	2130	-	24	1933	152	2116	-	24	1911
eng.rst.gum	165	20722	-	14	19496	24	2790	-	14	2617	24	2740	-	14	2575
eng.rst.rstdt	309	17646	-	17	16002	38	1797	-	17	1621	38	2346	-	17	2155
eng.sdrt.stac	33	9887	-	16	9580	6	1154	-	16	1145	6	1547	-	16	1510
eus.rst.ert	116	2785	-	29	2533	24	677	-	26	614	24	740	-	26	678
fas.rst.prstc	120	4607	-	17	4100	15	576	-	15	499	15	670	-	16	592
fra.sdrt.annodis	64	2255	-	18	2185	11	556	-	18	528	11	618	-	18	625
nld.rst.nldt	56	1662	-	32	1608	12	343	-	27	331	12	338	-	28	325
por.rst.cstn	114	4601	-	32	4148	14	630	-	22	573	12	306	-	21	272
rus.rst.rrt	272	34682	-	22	28868	30	3352	-	19	2855	30	3508	-	20	2843
spa.rst.rststb	203	2472	-	28	2240	32	419	-	23	383	32	460	-	25	426
spa.rst.sctb	32	473	-	24	439	9	103	-	17	94	9	168	-	19	159
zho.dep.scidtb	69	871	-	23	802	20	301	-	18	281	20	235	-	17	215
zho.rst.gcdt	40	7470	-	31	6454	5	1144	-	30	1006	5	1092	-	30	953
zho.rst.sctb	32	473	-	26	439	9	103	-	19	94	9	168	-	20	159
Tasks 2 and 3: Connective and Relations															
eng.pdtb.pdtb	1992	-	23850	23	43920	79	-	953	20	1674	91	-	1245	23	2257
***eng.pdtb.tedm**	-	-	-	-	-	2	-	110	20	178	4	-	231	18	351
ita.pdtb.luna	42	-	671	15	956	6	-	139	14	210	12	-	261	14	381
por.pdtb.crpc	243	-	3994	22	8797	28	-	621	20	1285	31	-	544	19	1248
***por.pdtb.tedm**	-	-	-	-	-	2	-	102	20	190	4	-	203	18	364
***tha.pdtb.tdtb**	139	-	8277	20	8278	19	-	1243	18	1243	22	-	1344	18	1344
tur.pdtb.tdb	159	-	7063	23	2451	19	-	831	22	312	19	-	854	22	422
***tur.pdtb.tedm**	-	-	-	-	-	2	-	135	21	213	4	-	247	22	364
zho.pdtb.cdtb	125	-	1034	9	3657	21	-	314	9	855	18	-	312	9	758

Table 1: Train / Dev / Test Statistics of DISRPT 2023 Datasets: **boldface** indicates a new corpus compared to DISRPT 2021, * indicates a surprise or an OOD dataset. '#Docs' and '#EDUs' correspond to the total number of documents and EDUs respectively. #Conn is the number of tokens starting a connective. '#Labels' corresponds to the size of the respective label set and '#Rels' to the total number of pairs annotated.

the smallest have about 50 documents and 15k tokens. We note that the Russian corpus has twice the amount of tokens compared to corpora of the same size in terms of documents, which indicates longer documents (scientific papers). The English SciDTB, on the other hand, is very large in document count, with almost 800 documents that seem very short: it is composed of scientific abstracts. In the lower part of Table 8 (PDTB framework), the difference is even more obvious: the English PDTB dataset contains 2,162 documents, while the English portion of the TED-Multilingual corpus only contains 6 documents (Zeyrek et al., 2018, 2019). In general, performance is lower for small datasets, and one way to improve performance when facing data scarcity is to take advantage of larger datasets, as attempted by some participants, notably for Task 3, relation classification.

The statistics also give insights into the differences between genres or languages and annotation guidelines across different corpora. The number of EDUs varies a lot: for example, the English STAC corpus contains a lot of EDUs relative to its size, likely due to the 'conversational' and abbreviated nature of online chatting. We can also see that the size of the label set differs between corpora, even within the same framework: between 9 and 23 for PDTB, 14 and 32 for RST, and 12 or 24 for DEP (SDRT has only 2 corpora with a more stable set of 16-18 labels). Label sets are not identical, even within the same framework, due to different relation definitions or granularity as well as variations in naming formats, e.g. with a single or a 2-level convention, as in CONCESSION vs COMPARISON.CONCESSION, or even more minor change such as the use of capital letters or not. Some datasets provide much more fine-grained relations (for example over 70 originally for RST-DT, or over 30 for GUM), but we follow the common practice of collapsing these to fewer coarse classes used in most parsing research (however, original fine-grained labels were retained in an additional column in the `.rels` files where available).

We count a total of 163 different relation names in the targeted level of granularity, which led one team to propose some mappings to reduce the label space. This situation is an important challenge when trying to experiment with joint learning across corpora, and points to an open research direction in increasing convergence of discourse relation labels in the field.

Finally, Table 1 provides the statistics for the splits of training, validation, and evaluation sets for each corpus. We indicate the size of the label set in each partition: unfortunately, in some corpora, some relations present in the training set are

Corpus	Treebanked: Gold / Stanza				Plain: Trankit			
	%Error		F1		%Error		F1	
	dev	test	dev	test	dev	test	dev	test
deu.rst.pcc^G	0.97	0.00	85.06	84.02	0.53	0.00	81.03	79.51
eng.dep.covdtb	0.00	0.00	59.35	57.16	0.27	0.35	58.03	55.71
eng.dep.scidtb	0.00	0.00	55.35	55.71	0.12	0.24	55.43	55.92
eng.rst.gum^G	0.00	0.00	60.88	60.95	0.25	1.19	60.11	59.31
eng.rst.rstdt^G	0.14	0.00	56.96	56.73	1.08	1.12	57.65	58.23
eng.sdrt.stac^G	0.30	0.30	92.12	92.63	3.95	3.36	62.54	57.49
eus.rst.ert	3.01	4.58	68.07	68.57	7.75	7.37	69.91	69.87
fas.rst.prstc	0.00	0.00	51.93	56.53	1.40	2.51	53.60	57.32
fra.sdrt.annodis	6.12	12.81	57.43	49.07	1.32	1.41	57.40	50.54
nld.rst.nldt	0.00	0.00	85.28	83.04	2.22	4.91	86.13	83.58
por.rst.cstn	0.39	0.00	57.72	62.47	0.39	0.72	57.88	61.71
rus.rst.rrt	21.53	19.74	59.11	59.89	27.97	25.44	57.46	58.30
spa.rst.rststb	0.00	0.70	75.48	76.31	0.00	0.37	72.64	73.35
spa.rst.sctb	3.95	3.51	81.56	78.01	4.29	3.92	77.46	72.59
zho.dep.scidtb	0.00	0.00	50.99	54.94	0.00	0.00	50.99	54.94
zho.rst.gcdt	0.00	0.00	44.88	46.95	0.35	0.35	39.52	41.48
zho.rst.sctb	6.98	7.52	84.66	81.73	8.33	9.82	75.43	72.14

Table 2: Sentence Segmentation Performance: each sentence beginning is annotated as an EDU boundary, baseline for segmentation (Task 1) computed on treebanked data (left) and .tok automatically split with Trankit (right), F1 scores on the dev and test partitions. Errors are the percentage of sentence beginnings not annotated as the beginning of an EDU (so an error of the sentence splitting). Corpora with gold sentences for the treebanked track are marked with a ^{G}.

not available in the evaluation set (e.g. 2 relations missing in `deu.rst.pcc`, 3 in `eus.rst.ert`, and 4 in `nld.rst.nldt`); even more crucially, in a few corpora, some relations are present in the test set but not in the dev set, preventing a good learning of these labels (`fas.rst.prstc`, `nld.rst.nldt`, and `por.rst.cstn`). This is another motivation for joint learning over different corpora; it could also be interesting to think about new splits of the data that would better preserve the label distribution.

4.3 Sentence and EDU Segmentation

Sentences are the basic unit for grouping words in NLP. They correspond to EDU boundaries: in most RST, SDRT, and DEP datasets each sentence starts a new EDU. With sentences given, the segmentation task corresponds to finding intra-sentential EDU boundaries, and corpora in general include these boundaries to some extent, depending possibly on the genre or the annotation scheme: for some corpora with a low rate of intra-sentential EDU boundaries, the task could thus be easier if the sentence splitter already gives good results. As a baseline and an indication of the complexity of the task, we thus report results for a sentence-based baseline, where each sentence is predicted to correspond to one EDU (see Table 2). We also report performance using another tool for sentence splitting, namely Trankit (Nguyen et al., 2021), used by the team MELODI for the Plain track.

Sentence boundaries are gold for some corpora (English RST-DT and GUM, and German PCC), for the others, Stanza (Qi et al., 2020) was used to provide sentence splits in the `.conllu` format (the Treebanked track). A `.tok` format is also provided, without information about sentences (the Plain track). Our baseline results are computed on the Treebanked data and shown in Table 2.

Error Rate: bad performance of sentence splitters We compute the error rate by looking at the tokens that are supposed to start a sentence but are not annotated as beginning an EDU: they thus correspond to errors in sentence segmentation. The error rate is not 0 for RST-DT (gold sentences), because of alignments errors with the Penn Treebank (Marcus et al., 1993). In addition, error rate is very high for the Russian corpus: 15% of the sentences do not correspond to a new EDU and thus are considered errors. The Russian RRT is composed of scientific papers containing lists of references annotated as one (very) large EDU while the tools tend to segment each reference as a separate sentence. We also have 'non-standard' sentences of the form "sci.comp_49-61" which might be figures. The error rate is also rather high for the e.g. French, Basque, Chinese, and Spanish corpora. The sentence splitter is clearly suboptimal for the French corpus, with errors due to e.g. lists or other uses of punctuations within sentences and also specific quotations marks, as shown in the examples below where curly brackets indicate predicted sentence boundaries:

- {Mais avec un Leica M7 , il est encore possible de dire : « Je fais de la photo !} {»} - *But with a Leica M7, it is still possible to say "I'm taking pictures!"*
- {En 1866 , le cartographe britannique Charles W.} {Wilson identifia les ruines de la synagogue (...)} - *In 1866, British cartographer Charles W. Wilson identified the ruins of the synagogue (...)*

High error rates could affect performance since sentences are generally the units fed to the systems, especially when the documents are too long for even large contextualized language models.

Baseline F-Score An F1 score gives an idea of one aspect of the complexity of the task: if F1 is high, it means that the corpus does not contain many intra-sentential EDU boundaries, which are arguably harder to detect. The STAC corpus mostly contains EDUs corresponding to a 'sentence', even if the definition of this unit is less clear for dialogues. The task should also be easier, with a good sentence splitter, for several RST corpora (nld, deu, zho, and spa). On the other hand, many corpora contain a high rate of intra-sentential EDUs, making the task harder, e.g. the Chinese SciDTB, the Farsi PRSTC, or the Chinese RST GCDT.

5 Participating Systems

Three teams submitted systems in time for participation: overall there were two systems for Tasks 1-2 and three systems for Task 3. All scores reported below come from our reproduction of these systems.

5.1 System Descriptions

HITS The HITS team participated in Tasks 1-2 and Tasks 3, with two separate systems. Their approach for Tasks 1 and 2 was language-specific, by fine-tuning monolingual or multilingual transformer-based models per corpus—for corpora with a training set. Their classifier architecture was based on pretrained models (various BERT or RoBERTa based for the monolingual models, XLM-RoBERTa-base for the multilingual), fine-tuned with a bidirectional LSTM network with a CRF layer (BiLSTM-CRF, Huang et al. 2015). They implemented an adversarial training strategy, which introduced small perturbations to the original inputs in order to help the trained model generalize better. For corpora without a training set (the surprise and OOD ones), they used their previously fine-tuned models of the same language and framework.

For Task 3, the team submitted a system composed of two fine-tuned transformer-based models (as in Tasks 1-2, BERT or RoBERTa based for the monolingual models, XLM-RoBERTa-base/large for the multilingual). For large corpora, a corpus-specific fine-tuned classifier was used, based on monolingual or multilingual models. However, they aggregated smaller corpora in a joint training approach based on their frameworks, and then fine-tuned a multilingual model for classification—and also used those for corpora without a training set. They also implemented the adversarial training strategy for this task, for specific datasets.

MELODI: DisCut and DiscReT The MELODI team submitted two systems to handle Tasks 1-2 and Task 3 respectively: DisCut and DiscReT. The former system is a revised version of the team's 2021 submission (Kamaladdini Ezzabady et al., 2021). The main modifications to DisCut included a shift to a single multilingual language model to accommodate all languages (XLM-RoBERTa-large was chosen, Conneau et al. 2020), and the use of a simple linear layer for classification, replacing the character-level CNN and token-level LSTM used in the 2021 version. Additionally, the team experimented with layer freezing, finding an overall optimum for the large language model when layers 0–5 of 24 were frozen. Both Tasks 1 and 2 were handled as BIO-encoded sequence labeling, and no additional features beyond sentence splits were used (for the plain text scenario, Trankit was used to preprocess the data, see Nguyen et al. 2021).

For Task 3, MELODI submitted DiscReT, which was unique in not only using a multilingual language model for all languages (this time choosing mBERT-base-cased) but also training jointly on all datasets after performing label lower-casing and selective merging to reduce the total of possible labels from 163 to 135 across datasets. Their models are fine-tuned and fitted with a fine-tuned Adapter. Adapters (Houlsby et al., 2019) offer a lightweight alternative built on transformers that expose only a subset of parameters to fine-tuning, reaching comparable results to fully fine-tuned transformers. The system did not use additional features, except for encoding the relation direction information by permuting the order of input sequences to always begin with the source argument of the relation (meaning sequences were transposed from their natural order for relations of the form 1<2).

DiscoFLAN DiscoFlan is based on the Flan-T5 generative language model, itself a fine-tuning of the T5 model on a large set of additional tasks (Chung et al., 2022). The basic principle of this family of models is to encode an instruction in natural language input to resolve a given NLP task, and to learn to decode it as the answer. In the case of discourse relation classification within DISRPT, this is implemented in DiscoFlan by fine-tuning Flan-T5 and encoding the instruction "what discourse relation holds between sent1 and sent2: sent1 <text> sent2 <text>" in various languages, and learning to decode the discourse relation label. A post-processing step tried to match an output token to an existing label, or select the majority class if the output cannot be mapped. The majority class is computed on the training set, or the dev set for the OOD corpora that do not have training sets.

corpus	track: Treebanked DisCut*			track: Treebanked HITS			track: Plain DisCut*		
	P	R	F1	P	R	F1	P	R	F1
deu.rst.pcc	97.88	94.22	96.01	97.58	95.92	**96.74**	96.77	91.84	94.24
****eng.dep.covdtb**	94.04	90.31	**92.13**	90.22	90.38	90.30	94.04	90.31	92.13
eng.dep.scidtb	94.96	95.18	**95.07**	94.77	95.09	94.93	94.94	94.05	94.49
eng.rst.gum	94.59	96.42	**95.50**	95.08	95.29	95.19	94.95	93.98	94.46
eng.rst.rstdt	97.21	98.04	**97.62**	96.46	97.66	97.06	96.70	98.81	97.74
eng.sdrt.stac	95.75	94.70	95.22	96.71	95.09	**95.89**	87.92	93.60	90.67
eus.rst.ert	88.18	91.76	89.93	90.14	90.14	**90.14**	89.66	92.57	91.09
fas.rst.prstc	94.92	91.94	**93.40**	92.95	92.54	92.74	93.29	93.43	93.36
fra.sdrt.annodis	88.06	88.35	**88.21**	88.82	87.38	88.09	91.34	90.45	90.89
nld.rst.nldt	98.17	94.97	**96.54**	93.62	91.12	92.35	97.05	97.34	97.19
por.rst.cstn	93.53	94.44	**93.98**	93.73	92.81	93.27	93.02	95.75	94.36
rus.rst.rrt	84.02	87.20	**85.58**	83.08	87.88	85.41	83.23	87.71	85.41
spa.rst.rststb	92.74	94.35	**93.53**	91.14	91.74	91.44	92.03	95.43	93.70
spa.rst.sctb	86.14	85.12	**85.63**	84.38	80.36	82.32	82.76	85.71	84.21
zho.dep.scidtb	83.58	95.32	89.07	84.00	98.3	**90.59**	84.64	96.17	90.04
zho.rst.gcdt	91.80	93.32	**92.55**	89.09	92.77	90.89	90.47	93.04	91.74
zho.rst.sctb	79.33	84.52	**81.84**	78.95	80.36	79.65	73.82	83.93	78.55
mean	91.46	92.36	**91.87**	90.63	91.46	**91.00**	**90.39**	**92.60**	**91.43**

Table 3: EDU Segmentation Results on Treebanked and Plain tracks: **boldface** indicates a new corpus compared to DISRPT 2021, and ** a surprise and OOD dataset. Disclosure: System marked with * was submitted by a team containing organizers and annotators of shared task datasets.

5.2 Results

Task 1: EDU Segmentation Table 3 shows the EDU Segmentation scores of the two submitted systems. The comparison between the two systems for the Treebanked track indicates very similar results, with the winner being DisCut (a mean F1 score of 91.87) from the MELODI team. Both systems used rather similar architectures, and the main difference was the language model used as backbone: always XLM-RoBERTa large for MELODI, and for HITS a language model was specifically chosen for the target language. As illustrated here, it seems that the hyper-parameter tuning including freezing layers and/or the use of a large version of RoBERTa allows performance to be on par with the specific base models. Major improvements were observed for `nld.rst.nldt` (MELODI +4 points), `spa.rst.rststb` (+2), `spa.rst.sctb` (+3), and `zho.rst.sctb` (+2). However, these variations should be taken with precaution as we noticed an important variance of the scores when reproducing the results, especially for small-sized corpora.

In general, scores are high, and the performance of DisCut is better than the ones obtained by the winning system DisCoDisCo in 2021 (Gessler et al., 2021), with a mean score of 91.77 when only considering the corpora used in 2021 against 91.48 for DisCoDisCo (for the Treebanked track). See the paper describing the MELODI results for a full comparison. Additionally, this year's mean scores are not far from the 2021 ones, despite the addition of the new corpora and one OOD dataset (`eng.dep.covdtb`). This demonstrates some robustness of the approaches as well as the consistencies of the new annotations. We note that a few corpora are still challenging, with performance below 90, in particular `rus.rst.rrt`, which is likely due to the issue with the bibliographic parts; and `spa.rst.sctb` and `zho.rst.sct`, which are parallel corpora and correspond to a rather high rate of sentence segmentation errors (4-7%), which should be investigated further.

The Plain track gives the opportunity to test EDU segmentation in a more realistic setting, i.e. no sentence splits are provided. However, since LLMs have severe limitations on input size, the DisCut system relies on another sentence segmentation, done with Trankit (Nguyen et al., 2021), but using the same tokenization as required for the evaluation for the shared task (which means that the results do not exactly reflect the performance of Trankit). Results show the mean performance is similar to the Treebanked track while, this time, no corpus contains gold sentence splits which is encouraging for future use of this kind of system on new data.

corpus	track: Treebanked DisCut*			track: Treebanked HITS			track: Plain DisCut*		
	P	**R**	**F1**	**P**	**R**	**F1**	**P**	**R**	**F1**
eng.pdtb.pdtb	95.49	91.89	93.66	93.61	94.06	**93.83**	94.08	89.32	91.64
****eng.pdtb.tedm**	82.69	74.46	78.36	81.74	77.49	**79.56**	83.77	69.26	75.83
ita.pdtb.luna	60.65	72.03	**65.85**	62.23	66.28	64.19	66.34	77.78	71.60
por.pdtb.crpc	80.81	80.51	80.66	80.59	80.88	**80.73**	78.49	80.51	79.49
****por.pdtb.tedm**	77.52	83.25	**80.29**	73.71	84.24	78.62	74.78	84.73	79.45
tha.pdtb.tdtb	84.24	87.13	85.66	85.74	87.2	**86.46**	85.32	59.23	69.92
tur.pdtb.tdb	92.34	93.21	92.77	92.3	95.43	**93.84**	90.33	91.92	91.12
****tur.pdtb.tedm**	87.41	50.61	64.10	91.49	52.23	**66.49**	51.01	88.73	64.78
zho.pdtb.cdtb	91.25	86.86	**89.00**	89.26	85.26	87.21	92.03	88.78	90.38
mean	82.64	79.14	80.17	82.68	79.73	**80.47**	**79.57**	**81.14**	**79.36**

Table 4: Connective Detection Results.

Task 2: Connective Detection Table 4 shows the connective detection results of the two submitted systems, which remain the same as for Task 1. We also observe similar scores between MELODI and HITS, but this time HITS is the winner (a mean F1 score of 80.47). Contrary to EDU segmentation, the new corpora added for this task are very challenging, especially the OOD ones coming from the TED multilingual corpus and the LUNA corpus, that are small and consist of documents from very specific genres (TED talks and speech transcriptions of dialogues). As a comparison, mean score of DisCoDisCo in 2021 was 91.22, while now the mean is around 80's. For this task, sentence segmentation seems less a crucial factor; however, the comparison between the two tracks demonstrate huge differences for some corpora, e.g. -5.75 for Luna and -15.74 for the Thai corpus when using Trankit vs Stanza. These differences should be investigated further to better assess the role of sentence splitting in connective detection.

Task 3: Relation Classification For the relation classification task, three systems were submitted: DiscReT, HITS, and DiscoFlan. The winning system is HITS, with a mean accuracy score of 62.36. The proposed strategy, with single models for large corpora and merging for small ones within each framework, seems more effective than the joint learning over all corpora proposed in DiscReT. Interestingly, the second system is still on par with or even better for a few corpora, meaning that merging across corpora to some extent could also help.

The scores indicate that some corpora are very challenging: the German PCC, the Turkish TDB, and the Dutch NLDT, with the accuracy score lower than 52. The new corpora do not seem more challenging than the others, except for the Turkish TEDm. We note that scores are very high for the Thai corpus (95.83), which could be due to the fact that only explicit relations are annotated in the current version. Compared to 2021, HITS has lower performance, with a mean accuracy score of 58.18 when only considering the corpora available in 2021 against 61.82 for DisCoDisCo, which indicates that the merging strategy including the new corpora could lead to drop in performance compared to single models, but more analysis is needed to investigate the impact of the hand-crafted features used in DisCoDisCo.

In order to provide more insights into the results, we also provide scores for implicit/explicit relations for some corpora, as shown in Table 6. Unexpectedly, we observe large differences in performance between explicit and implicit relations, with the latter having scores in the 40s against around 85 for the former. Some exceptions are high scores for implicit in the Portuguese CRPC and low scores for explicit in the Turkish TEDm. We also provide scores for each relation label for all corpora in Appendix C.

corpus	**DiscRet**	**HITS**	**DiscoFlan**
deu.rst.pcc	26.92	**31.92**	13.08
****eng.dep.covdtb**	41.30	**69.33**	50.15
eng.dep.scidtb	67.56	**74.15**	34.12
eng.pdtb.pdtb	69.25	**74.30**	24.41
****eng.pdtb.tedm**	19.94	**64.96**	33.05
eng.rst.gum	55.34	**68.19**	22.33
eng.rst.rstdt	49.98	**65.71**	36.94
eng.sdrt.stac	56.89	**60.79**	22.65
eus.rst.ert	51.77	**56.19**	28.02
fas.rst.prstc	50.34	**56.08**	25.84
fra.sdrt.annodis	44.96	**51.84**	19.36
ita.pdtb.luna	58.42	**65.00**	22.37
nld.rst.nldt	43.69	**51.69**	29.23
por.pdtb.crpc	72.76	**78.53**	43.83
****por.pdtb.tedm**	54.95	**64.84**	29.95
por.rst.cstn	62.87	**68.75**	38.60
rus.rst.rrt	**61.52**	60.99	23.60
spa.rst.rststb	**58.22**	57.28	26.76
spa.rst.sctb	33.33	**61.64**	44.65
tha.pdtb.tdtb	95.24	**95.83**	34.67
tur.pdtb.tdb	49.05	**45.50**	25.83
****tur.pdtb.tedm**	49.73	**54.12**	25.83
zho.dep.scidtb	**67.44**	**67.44**	33.49
zho.pdtb.cdtb	**69.13**	59.63	59.37
zho.rst.gcdt	55.72	**56.35**	20.46
zho.rst.sctb	49.06	**60.38**	43.40
mean	54.44	**62.36**	31.21

Table 5: Relation Classification Results on the Test Set.

corpus	DiscReT		HITS		#impl	#expl
	impl	expl	impl	expl		
eng.pdtb.pdtb	42.66	75.32	57.94	87.23	1008	1159
eng.pdtb.tedm	4.80	28.06	39.20	83.16	125	196
ita.pdtb.luna	17.21	62.02	49.18	72.48	122	258
por.pdtb.crpc	18.00	72.92	71.87	88.20	711	517
por.pdtb.tedm	15.85	69.95	42.68	85.25	164	183
tur.pdtb.tedm	22.95	52.40	44.26	59.62	122	208

Table 6: Implicit/Explicit Classification Results.

6 Conclusion

The DISRPT 2023 shared task was very challenging, with the addition of datasets from a new framework, in new languages, and 4 OOD surprise datasets without training partitions. The submitted systems still demonstrated rather high performance for EDU segmentation, with room for improvement for some corpora / languages / domains. However, further research and error analysis are needed to better understand not only what could be missing in the current models, but also what could be improved in some annotation projects, especially for example when EDU boundaries do not match sentence segmentation. Connective detection has been shown to be far from a solved task, with specific challenges for speech or dialogue data and generalizability to new domains. Finally, challenges are still significant for discourse relation classification. Competitors proposed original and attractive strategies to combine corpora due to data scarcity, but the label set explosion is a major obstacle as well as for analyzing the results. We hope that this work will bring new research and discussion in increasing convergence and cohesion of frameworks and annotation projects. We encourage researchers in the field to use the DISRPT data as a benchmark to evaluate their systems in the future in order to provide a realistic view of the robustness and generalization ability of their approaches.

Acknowledgements

This work is partially supported by the AnDiaMO project (ANR-21-CE23-0020) and the ANR (ANR-19-PI3A-0004) through the AI Interdisciplinary Institute, ANITI, as part of France's "Investing for the Future — PIA3" program.

This work is also partially supported by the SLANT project (ANR-19-CE23-0022) and the ANR grant SUMM-RE (ANR-20-CE23-0017). Chloé Braud and Philippe Muller are part of the programme DesCartes and are also supported by the National Research Foundation, Prime Minister's Office, Singapore under its Campus for Research Excellence and Technological Enterprise (CREATE) programme.

References

Stergos Afantenos, Nicholas Asher, Farah Benamara, Myriam Bras, Cécile Fabre, Mai Ho-dac, Anne Le Draoulec, Philippe Muller, Marie-Paule Péry-Woodley, Laurent Prévot, Josette Rebeyrolles, Ludovic Tanguy, Marianne Vergez-Couret, and Laure Vieu. 2012. An empirical resource for discovering cognitive principles of discourse organisation: the ANNODIS corpus. In *Proceedings of the Eighth International Conference on Language Resources and Evaluation (LREC'12)*, pages 2727–2734, Istanbul, Turkey. European Language Resources Association (ELRA).

Nicholas Asher, Julie Hunter, Mathieu Morey, Benamara Farah, and Stergos Afantenos. 2016. Discourse structure and dialogue acts in multiparty dialogue: the STAC corpus. In *Proceedings of the Tenth International Conference on Language Resources and Evaluation (LREC'16)*, pages 2721–2727, Portorož, Slovenia. European Language Resources Association (ELRA).

Nicholas Asher and Alex Lascarides. 2003. *Logics of Conversation*. Cambridge University Press, Cambridge.

Katherine Atwell, Anthony Sicilia, Seong Jae Hwang, and Malihe Alikhani. 2022. The change that matters in discourse parsing: Estimating the impact of domain shift on parser error. In *Findings of the Association for Computational Linguistics: ACL 2022*, pages 824–845, Dublin, Ireland. Association for Computational Linguistics.

Parminder Bhatia, Yangfeng Ji, and Jacob Eisenstein. 2015. Better document-level sentiment analysis from RST discourse parsing. In *Proceedings of the 2015 Conference on Empirical Methods in Natural Language Processing*, pages 2212–2218, Lisbon, Portugal. Association for Computational Linguistics.

Chloé Braud, Maximin Coavoux, and Anders Søgaard. 2017a. Cross-lingual RST discourse parsing. In *Proceedings of the 15th Conference of the European Chapter of the Association for Computational Linguistics: Volume 1, Long Papers*, pages 292–304, Valencia, Spain. Association for Computational Linguistics.

Chloé Braud, Ophélie Lacroix, and Anders Søgaard. 2017b. Cross-lingual and cross-domain discourse segmentation of entire documents. In *Proceedings of the 55th Annual Meeting of the Association for Computational Linguistics (Volume 2: Short Papers)*, pages 237–243, Vancouver, Canada. Association for Computational Linguistics.

Shuyuan Cao, Iria da Cunha, and Mikel Iruskieta. 2018. The RST Spanish-Chinese treebank. In *Proceedings of the Joint Workshop on Linguistic Annotation, Multiword Expressions and Constructions (LAW-MWE-CxG-2018)*, pages 156–166, Santa Fe, New Mexico, USA. Association for Computational Linguistics.

Paula Christina Figueira Cardoso, Erick Galani Maziero, Maria Lucía del Rosario Castro Jorge, M. Eloize, R. Kibar Aji Seno, Ariani Di Felippo, Lucia Helena Machado Rino, Maria das Graças Volpe Nunes, and Thiago Alexandre Salgueiro Pardo. 2011. CST-News - a discourse-annotated corpus for single and multi-document summarization of news texts in Brazilian Portuguese. In *Proceedings of the 3rd RST Brazilian Meeting*, pages 88–105, Cuiabá, Brazil.

Lynn Carlson and Daniel Marcu. 2001. Discourse tagging reference manual. Technical report, University of Southern California Information Sciences Institute.

Lynn Carlson, Daniel Marcu, and Mary Ellen Okurovsky. 2001. Building a discourse-tagged corpus in the framework of Rhetorical Structure Theory. In *Proceedings of the Second SIGdial Workshop on Discourse and Dialogue*.

Jiaao Chen and Diyi Yang. 2021. Structure-aware abstractive conversation summarization via discourse and action graphs. In *Proceedings of the 2021 Conference of the North American Chapter of the Association for Computational Linguistics: Human Language Technologies*, pages 1380–1391, Online. Association for Computational Linguistics.

Yi Cheng and Sujian Li. 2019. Zero-shot Chinese discourse dependency parsing via cross-lingual mapping. In *Proceedings of the 1st Workshop on Discourse Structure in Neural NLG*, pages 24–29, Tokyo, Japan. Association for Computational Linguistics.

Ta-Chung Chi and Alexander Rudnicky. 2022. Structured dialogue discourse parsing. In *Proceedings of the 23rd Annual Meeting of the Special Interest Group on Discourse and Dialogue*, pages 325–335, Edinburgh, UK. Association for Computational Linguistics.

Hyung Won Chung, Le Hou, Shayne Longpre, Barret Zoph, Yi Tay, William Fedus, Yunxuan Li, Xuezhi Wang, Mostafa Dehghani, Siddhartha Brahma, Albert Webson, Shixiang Shane Gu, Zhuyun Dai, Mirac Suzgun, Xinyun Chen, Aakanksha Chowdhery, Alex Castro-Ros, Marie Pellat, Kevin Robinson, Dasha Valter, Sharan Narang, Gaurav Mishra, Adams Yu, Vincent Zhao, Yanping Huang, Andrew Dai, Hongkun Yu, Slav Petrov, Ed H. Chi, Jeff Dean, Jacob Devlin, Adam Roberts, Denny Zhou, Quoc V. Le, and Jason Wei. 2022. Scaling instruction-finetuned language models.

Alexis Conneau, Kartikay Khandelwal, Naman Goyal, Vishrav Chaudhary, Guillaume Wenzek, Francisco Guzmán, Edouard Grave, Myle Ott, Luke Zettlemoyer, and Veselin Stoyanov. 2020. Unsupervised cross-lingual representation learning at scale. In *Proceedings of the 58th Annual Meeting of the Association for Computational Linguistics*, pages 8440–8451, Online. Association for Computational Linguistics.

Iria da Cunha, Juan-Manuel Torres-Moreno, and Gerardo Sierra. 2011. On the development of the RST Spanish treebank. In *Proceedings of the 5th Linguistic Annotation Workshop*, pages 1–10, Portland, Oregon, USA. Association for Computational Linguistics.

Nicolas Devatine, Philippe Muller, and Chloé Braud. 2022. Predicting political orientation in news with latent discourse structure to improve bias understanding. In *Proceedings of the 3rd Workshop on Computational Approaches to Discourse*, pages 77–85, Gyeongju, Republic of Korea and Online. International Conference on Computational Linguistics.

Jacob Devlin, Ming-Wei Chang, Kenton Lee, and Kristina Toutanova. 2019. BERT: Pre-training of deep bidirectional transformers for language understanding. In *Proceedings of the 2019 Conference of the North American Chapter of the Association for Computational Linguistics: Human Language Technologies, Volume 1 (Long and Short Papers)*, pages 4171–4186, Minneapolis, Minnesota. Association for Computational Linguistics.

Yaxin Fan, Peifeng Li, Fang Kong, and Qiaoming Zhu. 2022. A distance-aware multi-task framework for conversational discourse parsing. In *Proceedings of the 29th International Conference on Computational Linguistics*, pages 912–921, Gyeongju, Republic of Korea. International Committee on Computational Linguistics.

Vanessa Wei Feng. 2015. *RST-Style Discourse Parsing and Its Applications in Discourse Analysis*. Ph.D. thesis, University of Toronto.

Elisa Ferracane, Su Wang, and Raymond Mooney. 2017. Leveraging discourse information effectively for authorship attribution. In *Proceedings of the Eighth International Joint Conference on Natural Language Processing (Volume 1: Long Papers)*, pages 584–593, Taipei, Taiwan. Asian Federation of Natural Language Processing.

Michel Généreux, Iris Hendrickx, and Amália Mendes. 2012. Introducing the reference corpus of contemporary Portuguese online. In *Proceedings of the Eighth International Conference on Language Resources and Evaluation (LREC'12)*, pages 2237–2244, Istanbul, Turkey. European Language Resources Association (ELRA).

Luke Gessler, Shabnam Behzad, Yang Janet Liu, Siyao Peng, Yilun Zhu, and Amir Zeldes. 2021. DisCoDisCo at the DISRPT2021 shared task: A system for discourse segmentation, classification, and connective detection. In *Proceedings of the 2nd Shared Task on Discourse Relation Parsing and Treebanking (DISRPT 2021)*, pages 51–62, Punta Cana, Dominican Republic. Association for Computational Linguistics.

Freya Hewett and Manfred Stede. 2022. Extractive summarisation for German-language data: A text-level approach with discourse features. In *Proceedings of the 29th International Conference on Computational Linguistics*, pages 756–765, Gyeongju, Republic of Korea. International Committee on Computational Linguistics.

Tsutomu Hirao, Yasuhisa Yoshida, Masaaki Nishino, Norihito Yasuda, and Masaaki Nagata. 2013. Single-document summarization as a tree knapsack problem. In *Proceedings of the 2013 Conference on Empirical Methods in Natural Language Processing*, pages 1515–1520, Seattle, Washington, USA. Association for Computational Linguistics.

Neil Houlsby, Andrei Giurgiu, Stanislaw Jastrzebski, Bruna Morrone, Quentin De Laroussilhe, Andrea Gesmundo, Mona Attariyan, and Sylvain Gelly. 2019. Parameter-efficient transfer learning for NLP. In *International Conference on Machine Learning*, pages 2790–2799. PMLR.

Zhiheng Huang, Wei Xu, and Kai Yu. 2015. Bidirectional LSTM-CRF models for sequence tagging. *arXiv preprint arXiv:1508.01991*.

Patrick Huber and Giuseppe Carenini. 2020. From sentiment annotations to sentiment prediction through discourse augmentation. In *Proceedings of the 28th International Conference on Computational Linguistics*, pages 185–197, Barcelona, Spain (Online). International Committee on Computational Linguistics.

Mikel Iruskieta, María Jesús Aranzabe, Arantza Diaz de Ilarraza, Itziar Gonzalez-Dios, Mikel Lersundi, and Oier Lopez de Lacalle. 2013. The RST Basque TreeBank: An online search interface to check rhetorical relations. In *4th Workshop on RST and Discourse Studies*, pages 40–49, Fortaleza, Brasil.

Mikel Iruskieta, Iria Cunha, and Maite Taboada. 2015. A qualitative comparison method for rhetorical structures: Identifying different discourse structures in multilingual corpora. *Language Resources and Evaluation*, 49(2):263–309.

Anders Johannsen and Anders Søgaard. 2013. Disambiguating explicit discourse connectives without oracles. In *Proceedings of the Sixth International Joint Conference on Natural Language Processing*, pages 997–1001, Nagoya, Japan. Asian Federation of Natural Language Processing.

Shafiq Joty, Francisco Guzmán, Lluís Màrquez, and Preslav Nakov. 2017. Discourse structure in machine translation evaluation. *Computational Linguistics*, 43(4):683–722.

Morteza Kamaladdini Ezzabady, Philippe Muller, and Chloé Braud. 2021. Multi-lingual discourse segmentation and connective identification: MELODI at disrpt2021. In *Proceedings of the 2nd Shared Task on Discourse Relation Parsing and Treebanking (DISRPT 2021)*, pages 22–32, Punta Cana, Dominican Republic. Association for Computational Linguistics.

Hamid Karimi and Jiliang Tang. 2019. Learning hierarchical discourse-level structure for fake news detection. In *Proceedings of the 2019 Conference of the North American Chapter of the Association for Computational Linguistics: Human Language Technologies, Volume 1 (Long and Short Papers)*, pages 3432–3442, Minneapolis, Minnesota. Association for Computational Linguistics.

Najoung Kim, Song Feng, Chulaka Gunasekara, and Luis Lastras. 2020. Implicit discourse relation classification: We need to talk about evaluation. In *Proceedings of the 58th Annual Meeting of the Association for Computational Linguistics*, pages 5404–5414, Online. Association for Computational Linguistics.

Naoki Kobayashi, Tsutomu Hirao, Hidetaka Kamigaito, Manabu Okumura, and Masaaki Nagata. 2022. A simple and strong baseline for end-to-end neural RST-style discourse parsing. In *Findings of the Association for Computational Linguistics: EMNLP 2022*, pages 6725–6737, Abu Dhabi, United Arab Emirates. Association for Computational Linguistics.

Li Liang, Zheng Zhao, and Bonnie Webber. 2020. Extending implicit discourse relation recognition to the PDTB-3. In *Proceedings of the First Workshop on Computational Approaches to Discourse*, pages 135–147, Online. Association for Computational Linguistics.

Yang Liu, Ivan Titov, and Mirella Lapata. 2019. Single document summarization as tree induction. In *Proceedings of the 2019 Conference of the North American Chapter of the Association for Computational Linguistics: Human Language Technologies, Volume 1 (Long and Short Papers)*, pages 1745–1755, Minneapolis, Minnesota. Association for Computational Linguistics.

Yang Janet Liu and Amir Zeldes. 2023. Why can't discourse parsing generalize? a thorough investigation of the impact of data diversity. In *Proceedings of the 17th Conference of the European Chapter of the Association for Computational Linguistics*, pages 3112–3130, Dubrovnik, Croatia. Association for Computational Linguistics.

Zhengyuan Liu and Nancy Chen. 2021. Improving multi-party dialogue discourse parsing via domain integration. In *Proceedings of the 2nd Workshop on Computational Approaches to Discourse*, pages 122–127, Punta Cana, Dominican Republic and Online. Association for Computational Linguistics.

Zhengyuan Liu, Ke Shi, and Nancy Chen. 2020. Multilingual neural RST discourse parsing. In *Proceedings of the 28th International Conference on Computational Linguistics*, pages 6730–6738, Barcelona, Spain (Online). International Committee on Computational Linguistics.

Zhengyuan Liu, Ke Shi, and Nancy Chen. 2021. DMRST: A joint framework for document-level multilingual RST discourse segmentation and parsing. In *Proceedings of the 2nd Workshop on Computational Approaches to Discourse*, pages 154–164, Punta Cana, Dominican Republic and Online. Association for Computational Linguistics.

Wanqiu Long and Bonnie Webber. 2022. Facilitating contrastive learning of discourse relational senses by exploiting the hierarchy of sense relations. In *Proceedings of the 2022 Conference on Empirical Methods in Natural Language Processing*, pages 10704–10716, Abu Dhabi, United Arab Emirates. Association for Computational Linguistics.

Annie Louis, Aravind Joshi, and Ani Nenkova. 2010. Discourse indicators for content selection in summarization. In *Proceedings of the SIGDIAL 2010 Conference*, pages 147–156, Tokyo, Japan. Association for Computational Linguistics.

William C. Mann and Sandra A. Thompson. 1988. Rhetorical Structure Theory: Toward a functional theory of text organization. *Text*, 8:243–281.

Mitchell P. Marcus, Beatrice Santorini, and Mary Ann Marcinkiewicz. 1993. Building a large annotated corpus of english: The penn treebank. *Special Issue on Using Large Corpora, Computational Linguistics*, 19(2):313–330.

Amália Mendes and Pierre Lejeune. 2022. Crpc-db a discourse bank for portuguese. In *Computational Processing of the Portuguese Language: 15th International Conference, PROPOR 2022, Fortaleza, Brazil, March 21–23, 2022, Proceedings*, page 79–89, Berlin, Heidelberg. Springer-Verlag.

Philippe Muller, Stergos Afantenos, Pascal Denis, and Nicholas Asher. 2012. Constrained decoding for text-level discourse parsing. In *Proceedings of COLING 2012*, pages 1883–1900, Mumbai, India. The COLING 2012 Organizing Committee.

Philippe Muller, Chloé Braud, and Mathieu Morey. 2019. ToNy: Contextual embeddings for accurate multilingual discourse segmentation of full documents. In *Proceedings of the Workshop on Discourse Relation Parsing and Treebanking 2019*, pages 115–124, Minneapolis, MN. Association for Computational Linguistics.

Minh Van Nguyen, Viet Dac Lai, Amir Pouran Ben Veyseh, and Thien Huu Nguyen. 2021. Trankit: A light-weight transformer-based toolkit for multilingual natural language processing. In *Proceedings of the 16th Conference of the European Chapter of the Association for Computational Linguistics: System Demonstrations*, pages 80–90, Online. Association for Computational Linguistics.

Noriki Nishida and Yuji Matsumoto. 2022. Out-of-domain discourse dependency parsing via bootstrapping: An empirical analysis on its effectiveness and limitation. *Transactions of the Association for Computational Linguistics*, 10:127–144.

Siyao Peng, Yang Janet Liu, and Amir Zeldes. 2022a. Chinese Discourse Annotation Reference Manual. Research Report, Georgetown University (Washington, D.C.).

Siyao Peng, Yang Janet Liu, and Amir Zeldes. 2022b. GCDT: A Chinese RST Treebank for Multigenre and Multilingual Discourse Parsing. In *Proceedings of the 2nd Conference of the Asia-Pacific Chapter of the Association for Computational Linguistics and the 12th International Joint Conference on Natural Language Processing*, pages 382–391, Online only. Association for Computational Linguistics.

Emily Pitler, Mridhula Raghupathy, Hena Mehta, Ani Nenkova, Alan Lee, and Aravind Joshi. 2008. Easily identifiable discourse relations. In *Coling 2008: Companion volume: Posters*, pages 87–90, Manchester, UK. Coling 2008 Organizing Committee.

Rashmi Prasad, Aravind Joshi, Nikhil Dinesh, Alan Lee, Eleni Miltsakaki, and Bonnie Webber. 2005. The Penn Discourse TreeBank as a resource for natural language generation. In *Proceedings of the Corpus Linguistics Workshop on Using Corpora for Natural Language Generation*, pages 25–32.

Rashmi Prasad, Bonnie Webber, and Aravind Joshi. 2014. Reflections on the Penn Discourse TreeBank, comparable corpora, and complementary annotation. *Computational Linguistics*, 40(4):921–950.

Dongqi Pu, Yifan Wang, and Vera Demberg. 2023. Incorporating distributions of discourse structure for long document abstractive summarization. In *Proceedings of ACL 2023*, Toronto, Canada.

Peng Qi, Yuhao Zhang, Yuhui Zhang, Jason Bolton, and Christopher D. Manning. 2020. Stanza: A Python natural language processing toolkit for many human languages. In *Proceedings of the 58th Annual Meeting of the Association for Computational Linguistics: System Demonstrations*.

Gisela Redeker, Ildikó Berzlánovich, Nynke van der Vliet, Gosse Bouma, and Markus Egg. 2012. Multi-layer discourse annotation of a Dutch text corpus. In *Proceedings of the Eighth International Conference on Language Resources and Evaluation (LREC'12)*, pages 2820–2825, Istanbul, Turkey. European Language Resources Association (ELRA).

Giuseppe Riccardi, Evgeny A. Stepanov, and Shammur Absar Chowdhury. 2016. Discourse connective detection in spoken conversations. In *2016 IEEE International Conference on Acoustics, Speech and Signal Processing (ICASSP)*, pages 6095–6099.

Merel Scholman, Tianai Dong, Frances Yung, and Vera Demberg. 2021. Comparison of methods for explicit discourse connective identification across various domains. In *Proceedings of the 2nd Workshop on Computational Approaches to Discourse*, pages 95–106, Punta Cana, Dominican Republic and Online. Association for Computational Linguistics.

Sara Shahmohammadi, Hadi Veisi, and Ali Darzi. 2021. Persian Rhetorical Structure Theory. *arXiv preprint arXiv:2106.13833*.

Manfred Stede and Arne Neumann. 2014. Potsdam commentary corpus 2.0: Annotation for discourse research. In *Proceedings of the Ninth International Conference on Language Resources and Evaluation (LREC'14)*, pages 925–929, Reykjavik, Iceland. European Language Resources Association (ELRA).

Svetlana Toldova, Dina Pisarevskaya, Margarita Ananyeva, Maria Kobozeva, Alexander Nasedkin, Sofia Nikiforova, Irina Pavlova, and Alexey Shelepov. 2017. Rhetorical relations markers in Russian RST treebank. In *Proceedings of the 6th Workshop on Recent Advances in RST and Related Formalisms*, pages 29–33, Santiago de Compostela, Spain. Association for Computational Linguistics.

Sara Tonelli, Giuseppe Riccardi, Rashmi Prasad, and Aravind Joshi. 2010. Annotation of discourse relations for conversational spoken dialogs. In *Proceedings of the Seventh International Conference on Language Resources and Evaluation (LREC'10)*, Valletta, Malta. European Language Resources Association (ELRA).

Mei Tu, Yu Zhou, and Chengqing Zong. 2013. A novel translation framework based on Rhetorical Structure Theory. In *Proceedings of the 51st Annual Meeting of the Association for Computational Linguistics (Volume 2: Short Papers)*, pages 370–374, Sofia, Bulgaria. Association for Computational Linguistics.

Bonnie Webber, Andrei Popescu-Belis, Katja Markert, and Jörg Tiedemann, editors. 2013. *Proceedings of the Workshop on Discourse in Machine Translation*. Association for Computational Linguistics, Sofia, Bulgaria.

Ngo Xuan Bach, Nguyen Le Minh, and Akira Shimazu. 2012. A reranking model for discourse segmentation using subtree features. In *Proceedings of the 13th Annual Meeting of the Special Interest Group on Discourse and Dialogue*, pages 160–168, Seoul, South Korea. Association for Computational Linguistics.

Nianwen Xue, Hwee Tou Ng, Sameer Pradhan, Attapol Rutherford, Bonnie Webber, Chuan Wang, and Hongmin Wang. 2016. CoNLL 2016 shared task on multilingual shallow discourse parsing. In *Proceedings of the CoNLL-16 shared task*, pages 1–19, Berlin, Germany. Association for Computational Linguistics.

An Yang and Sujian Li. 2018. SciDTB: Discourse dependency TreeBank for scientific abstracts. In *Proceedings of the 56th Annual Meeting of the Association for Computational Linguistics (Volume 2: Short Papers)*, pages 444–449, Melbourne, Australia. Association for Computational Linguistics.

Cheng Yi, Li Sujian, and Li Yueyuan. 2021. Unifying discourse resources with dependency framework. In *Proceedings of the 20th Chinese National Conference on Computational Linguistics*, pages 1058–1065, Huhhot, China. Chinese Information Processing Society of China.

Yasuhisa Yoshida, Jun Suzuki, Tsutomu Hirao, and Masaaki Nagata. 2014. Dependency-based discourse parser for single-document summarization. In *Proceedings of the 2014 Conference on Empirical Methods in Natural Language Processing (EMNLP)*, pages 1834–1839, Doha, Qatar. Association for Computational Linguistics.

Nan Yu, Guohong Fu, and Min Zhang. 2022a. Speaker-aware discourse parsing on multi-party dialogues. In *Proceedings of the 29th International Conference on Computational Linguistics*, pages 5372–5382, Gyeongju, Republic of Korea. International Committee on Computational Linguistics.

Nan Yu, Meishan Zhang, Guohong Fu, and Min Zhang. 2022b. RST discourse parsing with second-stage EDU-level pre-training. In *Proceedings of the 60th Annual Meeting of the Association for Computational Linguistics (Volume 1: Long Papers)*, pages 4269–4280, Dublin, Ireland. Association for Computational Linguistics.

Amir Zeldes. 2017. The GUM Corpus: Creating Multilayer Resources in the Classroom. *Language Resources and Evaluation*, 51(3):581–612.

Amir Zeldes, Debopam Das, Erick Galani Maziero, Juliano Antonio, and Mikel Iruskieta. 2019. The DISRPT 2019 shared task on elementary discourse unit segmentation and connective detection. In *Proceedings of the Workshop on Discourse Relation Parsing and Treebanking 2019*, pages 97–104, Minneapolis, MN. Association for Computational Linguistics.

Amir Zeldes, Yang Janet Liu, Mikel Iruskieta, Philippe Muller, Chloé Braud, and Sonia Badene. 2021. The DISRPT 2021 shared task on elementary discourse unit segmentation, connective detection, and relation classification. In *Proceedings of the 2nd Shared Task on Discourse Relation Parsing and Treebanking (DISRPT 2021)*, pages 1–12, Punta Cana, Dominican Republic. Association for Computational Linguistics.

Deniz Zeyrek and Murathan Kurfalı. 2017. TDB 1.1: Extensions on Turkish discourse bank. In *Proceedings of the 11th Linguistic Annotation Workshop*, pages 76–81, Valencia, Spain. Association for Computational Linguistics.

Deniz Zeyrek, Amália Mendes, Yulia Grishina, Murathan Kurfalı, Samuel Gibbon, and Maciej Ogrodniczuk. 2019. TED Multilingual Discourse Bank (TED-MDB): A parallel corpus annotated in the PDTB style. *Language Resources and Evaluation*, pages 1–27.

Deniz Zeyrek, Amália Mendes, and Murathan Kurfalı. 2018. Multilingual extension of PDTB-style annotation: The case of TED multilingual discourse bank. In *Proceedings of the Eleventh International Conference on Language Resources and Evaluation (LREC 2018)*, Miyazaki, Japan. European Language Resources Association (ELRA).

Deniz Zeyrek and Bonnie Webber. 2008. A discourse resource for Turkish: Annotating discourse connectives in the METU corpus. In *Proceedings of the 6th Workshop on Asian Language Resources*.

Yuping Zhou, Jill Lu, Jennifer Zhang, and Nianwen Xue. 2014. Chinese Discourse Treebank 0.5 LDC2014T21.

A Relation Mapping Details

Table 7 provides the mapping done for the relation labels in addition to translation to English when needed. A few cases of labels were also removed when they did not correspond to a discourse relation.

Corpus	Original label	Mapped label
eus.rst.ert	anthitesis	antithesis
	motibation	motivation
	solution-hood	solutionhood
spa.rst.rststb	backgroun	background
fas.rst.prstc	topicomment	topic-comment
	topichange	topic-change
	topidrift	topic-drift
por.rst.cstn	non-volitional-cause	nonvolitional-cause
	non-volitional-cause-e	nonvolitional-cause-e
	non-volitional-result	nonvolitional-result
	non-volitional-result-e	nonvolitional-result-e
deu.rst.pcc	e-elab	e-elaboration
fra.sdrt.annodis	e-elab	e-elaboration
nld.rst.nldt	span	relation removed
eng.dep.scidtb	null	relation removed
ita.pdtb.luna	null	relation removed

Table 7: Relation Mapping used in DISRPT 2023.

B DISRPT 2023 Corpora Statistics

Table 8 provides detailed statistics on all DISRPT 2023 corpora regarding their sizes and properties.

Corpus	Domain	mwt	#Docs	#Sents	#Tokens	Vocab	#EDUs	#Conn	#Labels	#Rels	References
				Tasks 1 and 3: EDU Segmentation and Relation Classification							
deu.rst.pcc	newspaper commentaries	n	176	2,193	33,222	8,359	3,018	-	26	2,665	Potsdam Commentary Corpus (Stede and Neumann, 2014)
****eng.dep.covdtb**	scholarly paper abstracts on COVID-19 and related coronaviruses	y	300	2,343	60,849	8,293	5,705	-	12	4,985	COVID-19 Discourse Dependency Treebank (COVID19-DTB) (Nishida and Matsumoto, 2022)
eng.dep.scidtb	scientific articles	y	798	4,202	102,493	8,700	10,986	-	24	9,904	Discourse Dependency TreeBank for Scientific Abstracts (SciDTB) (Yang and Li, 2018)
eng.rst.gum	multi-genre	y	213	11,656	203,879	19,404	26,252	-	14	24,688	Georgetown University Multi-layer corpus V9 (Zeldes, 2017)
eng.rst.rstdt	news	y	385	8,318	205,829	19,160	21,789	-	17	19,778	RST Discourse Treebank (Carlson et al., 2001)
eng.sdrt.stac	dialogues	y	45	11,087	52,354	3,967	12,588	-	16	12,235	Strategic Conversations corpus (Asher et al., 2016)
eus.rst.ert	medical, terminological and scientific	n	164	2,380	45,780	13,662	4,202	-	29	3,825	Basque RST Treebank (Iruskieta et al., 2013)
fas.rst.prstc	journalistic texts	y	150	2,179	66,694	7,880	5,853	-	17	5,191	Persian RST Corpus (Shahmohammadi et al., 2021)
fra.sdrt.annodis	news, wiki	n	86	1,507	32,699	7,513	3,429	-	18	3,338	ANNOtation DIScursive (Afantenos et al., 2012).
nld.rst.nldt	expository texts and persuasive genres	n	80	1,651	24,898	4,935	2,343	-	32	2,264	Dutch Discourse Treebank (Redeker et al., 2012)
por.rst.cstn	news	y	140	2,221	58,793	7,786	5,537	-	32	4,993	Cross-document Structure Theory News Corpus (Cardoso et al., 2011)
rus.rst.rrt	blog and news	n	332	23,044	473,005	75,285	41,542	-	22	34,566	Russian RST Treebank (Toldova et al., 2017)
spa.rst.rststb	multi-genre	n	267	2,089	58,717	9,444	3,351	-	28	3,049	RST Spanish Treebank (da Cunha et al., 2011)
spa.rst.sctb	multi-genre	n	50	516	16,515	3,735	744	-	25	692	RST Spanish-Chinese Treebank (Spanish) (Cao et al., 2018)
zho.dep.scidtb	scientific	n	109	609	18,761	2,427	1,407	-	23	1,298	Discourse Dependency TreeBank for Scientific Abstracts (SciDTB) (Yi et al., 2021; Cheng and Li, 2019)
zho.rst.gcdt	multi-genre	n	50	2,692	62,905	9,818	9,706	-	31	8,413	Georgetown Chinese Discourse Treebank (GCDT) (Peng et al., 2022b,a)
zho.rst.sctb	multi-genre	n	50	580	15,496	2,973	744	-	26	692	RST Spanish-Chinese Treebank (Chinese) (Cao et al., 2018)
				Tasks 2 and 3: Connective Detection and Relation Classification							
eng.pdtb.pdtb	news	y	2,162	48,630	1,156,657	48,937	-	26,048	23	47,851	Penn Discourse Treebank (Prasad et al., 2014)
****eng.pdtb.tedm**	TED talks	y	6	381	8,048	1,881	-	341	20	529	TED-Multilingual Discourse Bank (English) (Zeyrek et al., 2018, 2019)
ita.pdtb.luna	speech	y	60	3,753	26,114	2,392	-	1,071	16	1,547	LUNA Corpus Discourse Data Set (Tonelli et al., 2010; Riccardi et al., 2016)
por.pdtb.crpc[5]	news, fiction, and didactic/scientific texts	n	302	5,194	186,849	22,208	-	5,159	22	11,330	Portuguese Discourse Bank (CRPC) (Mendes and Lejeune, 2022; Généreux et al., 2012)
****por.pdtb.tedm**	TED talks	n	6	394	8,190	2,162	-	305	20	554	TED-Multilingual Discourse Bank (Portuguese) (Zeyrek et al., 2018, 2019)
***tha.pdtb.tdtb**	news	n	180	6,534	256,523	11,789	-	10,864	21	10,865	Thai Discourse Treebank (TDTB)
tur.pdtb.tdb	multi-genre	y	197	31,196	487,389	88,923	-	8,748	23	3,185	Turkish Discourse Bank (Zeyrek and Webber, 2008; Zeyrek and Kurfalı, 2017)
****tur.pdtb.tedm**	TED talks	y	6	410	6,143	2,771	-	382	23	577	TED-Multilingual Discourse Bank (Turkish) (Zeyrek et al., 2018, 2019)
zho.pdtb.cdtb	news	n	164	2,891	73,314	9,085	-	1,660	9	5,270	Chinese Discourse Treebank (Zhou et al., 2014)

Table 8: General Statistics of DISRPT 2023 Datasets: **boldface** indicates a new corpus compared to DISRPT 2021, $*$ indicates a surprise dataset and $**$ a surprise and OOD dataset. 'mwt' corresponds to the annotation ('y') or not ('n') of multi-word expressions. '#Docs', '#Sents', '#Tokens' and '#EDUs' correspond to the total number of documents, sentences (the Treebanked track), tokens, and EDUs respectively. #Conn is the number of tokens starting a connective. 'Vocab' is the number of unique tokens. '#Labels' corresponds to the size of the respective label set and '#Rels' to the total number of pairs annotated.

C Relation Scores Per Label

Tables below provide a detailed breakdown of the accuracy scores for each corpus and each label for the discourse relation classification task (i.e. Task 3). The results of the HITS and the DiscReT systems are presented.

	HITS			DiscReT			
deu.rst.pcc	P	R	F1	P	R	F1	Num.
antithesis	36.36	22.22	27.59	16.67	5.56	8.33	1800
background	16.67	11.76	13.79	0.00	0.00	0.00	1700
cause	25.00	100	40.00	0.00	0.00	0.00	200
circumstance	33.33	6.67	11.11	42.86	20.00	27.27	1500
concession	31.25	38.46	34.48	30.77	30.77	30.77	1300
condition	58.33	77.78	66.67	0.00	0.00	0.00	900
conjunction	33.33	57.14	42.11	0.00	0.00	0.00	700
contrast	16.67	12.50	14.29	0.00	0.00	0.00	800
e-elaboration	69.23	81.82	75.00	60.00	54.55	57.14	1100
elaboration	24.00	60.00	34.29	8.33	20.00	11.76	1000
evaluation-n	0.00	0.00	0.00	0.00	0.00	0.00	300
evaluation-s	0.00	0.00	0.00	0.00	0.00	0.00	1700
evidence	50.00	20.00	28.57	0.00	0.00	0.00	1000
interpretation	0.00	0.00	0.00	11.11	41.67	17.54	1200
joint	14.29	13.79	14.04	8.33	6.90	7.55	2900
list	42.42	53.85	47.46	59.09	50.00	54.17	2600
means	100	50.00	66.67	0.00	0.00	0.00	200
preparation	28.57	50.00	36.36	14.29	25.00	18.18	400
purpose	100	100	100	50.00	66.67	57.14	300
reason	52.00	38.24	44.07	43.33	38.24	40.62	3400
restatement	0.00	0.00	0.00	0.00	0.00	0.00	100
sequence	75.00	42.86	54.55	0.00	0.00	0.00	700
solutionhood	0.00	0.00	0.00	0.00	0.00	0.00	100
summary	0.00	0.00	0.00	0.00	0.00	0.00	100
macro avg	33.60	34.88	31.29	14.37	14.97	13.77	26000
weighted avg	33.51	31.92	30.72	21.84	20.00	19.88	26000

	HITS			DiscReT			
eng.dep.covdtb	P	R	F1	P	R	F1	Num.
ATTRIBUTION	92.52	96.12	94.29	95.28	98.06	96.65	10300
BACKGROUND	61.02	82.44	70.13	0.00	0.00	0.00	13100
CAUSE-RESULT	57.73	41.48	48.28	0.00	0.00	0.00	13500
COMPARISON	83.33	13.07	22.60	84.00	13.73	23.60	15300
CONDITION	65.00	59.09	61.90	0.00	0.00	0.00	2200
ELABORATION	80.27	81.26	80.77	85.25	46.34	60.04	129700
ENABLEMENT	93.17	86.43	89.67	97.03	44.34	60.87	22100
FINDINGS	0.00	0.00	0.00	0.00	0.00	0.00	15400
JOINT	58.96	90.29	71.33	33.15	67.43	44.44	17500
MANNER-MEANS	80.43	64.35	71.50	83.64	40.00	54.12	11500
TEMPORAL	64.52	80.00	71.43	75.00	12.00	20.69	2500
TEXTUAL-ORGANIZATION	0.00	0.00	0.00	0.00	0.00	0.00	5500
macro avg	61.41	57.88	56.82	46.11	26.82	30.03	258600
weighted avg	71.69	69.33	68.56	66.50	38.21	46.17	258600

	HITS			DiscReT			
eng.dep.scidtb	P	R	F1	P	R	F1	Num.
attribution	94.78	96.95	95.85	95.38	94.66	95.02	13100
bg-compare	82.35	60.87	70.00	60.00	39.13	47.37	4600
bg-general	71.74	89.19	79.52	87.18	91.89	89.47	3700
bg-goal	52.11	66.07	58.27	33.33	62.50	43.48	5600
cause	33.33	36.36	34.78	0.00	0.00	0.00	1100
comparison	57.89	52.38	55.00	92.86	61.90	74.29	2100
condition	83.33	60.61	70.18	0.00	0.00	0.00	3300
contrast	72.29	84.51	77.92	0.00	0.00	0.00	7100
elab-addition	77.65	75.15	76.38	78.76	69.94	74.09	65200
elab-aspect	18.67	31.11	23.33	11.20	31.11	16.47	4500
elab-definition	20.00	25.00	22.22	0.00	0.00	0.00	400
elab-enumember	85.71	62.07	72.00	71.43	68.97	70.18	2900
elab-example	78.26	52.94	63.16	88.89	47.06	61.54	3400
elab-process_step	52.00	44.83	48.15	40.00	48.28	43.75	2900
enablement	77.04	81.89	79.39	79.67	77.17	78.40	12700
evaluation	81.62	84.83	83.20	71.26	69.66	70.45	17800
exp-evidence	70.00	53.85	60.87	0.00	0.00	0.00	1300
exp-reason	91.67	78.57	84.62	77.78	50.00	60.87	1400
joint	83.77	82.69	83.23	74.05	87.82	80.35	15600
manner-means	86.61	80.17	83.26	90.57	79.34	84.58	12100
progression	42.11	33.33	37.21	12.50	2.08	3.57	4800
result	30.77	25.81	28.07	0.00	0.00	0.00	3100
summary	0.00	0.00	0.00	0.00	0.00	0.00	100
temporal	55.56	86.96	67.80	60.87	60.87	60.87	2300
weighted avg	75.22	74.15	74.35	67.40	63.89	64.92	191100
macro avg	62.47	60.26	60.60	46.91	43.43	43.95	191100

	HITS			DiscReT			
eng.pdtb.pdtb	P	R	F1	P	R	F1	Num.
Comparison. Concession	85.71	75.22	80.13	74.78	76.12	75.44	33500
Comparison. Concession+ SpeechAct	0.00	0.00	0.00	0.00	0.00	0.00	200
Comparison. Contrast	65.62	62.69	64.12	68.48	47.01	55.75	13400
Comparison. Similarity	90.00	81.82	85.71	66.67	72.73	69.57	1100
Contingency.Cause	76.96	68.27	72.36	67.59	70.19	68.87	41600
Contingency.Cause+ Belief	11.11	13.33	12.12	0.00	0.00	0.00	1500
Contingency.Cause+ SpeechAct	0.00	0.00	0.00	0.00	0.00	0.00	300
Contingency. Condition	81.93	89.47	85.53	84.85	73.68	78.87	7600
Contingency. Condition+ SpeechAct	25.00	12.50	16.67	0.00	0.00	0.00	800
Contingency. Negative-cause	100	100	100	0.00	0.00	0.00	100
Contingency. Negative-condition	100	100	100	100	50.00	66.67	200
Contingency.Purpose	73.33	71.74	72.53	78.95	65.22	71.43	4600
Expansion. Conjunction	74.50	88.57	80.93	79.96	78.95	79.45	55100
Expansion. Disjunction	64.29	100	78.26	0.00	0.00	0.00	900
Expansion. Equivalence	30.77	16.67	21.62	0.00	0.00	0.00	2400
Expansion.Exception	0.00	0.00	0.00	0.00	0.00	0.00	100
Expansion. Instantiation	71.84	74.75	73.27	72.92	70.71	71.79	9900
Expansion.Level-of-detail	63.33	56.72	59.84	0.00	0.00	0.00	20100
Expansion.Manner	69.23	90.00	78.26	71.15	92.50	80.43	4000
Expansion. Substitution	86.67	66.67	75.36	85.71	46.15	60.00	3900
Hypophora	72.73	100	84.21	0.00	0.00	0.00	800
Temporal. Asynchronous	81.89	74.29	77.90	81.51	69.29	74.90	14000
Temporal. Synchronous	67.24	81.25	73.58	0.00	0.00	0.00	9600
weighted avg	74.28	74.30	73.88	63.02	60.35	61.37	225700
macro avg	60.53	61.91	60.54	40.55	35.33	37.09	225700

	HITS			DiscReT			
eng.pdtb.tedm	P	R	F1	P	R	F1	Num.
Comparison. Concession	62.16	88.46	73.02	52.38	42.31	46.81	2600
Comparison. Contrast	80.00	30.77	44.44	50.00	15.38	23.53	1300
Comparison. Similarity	50.00	28.57	36.36	0.00	0.00	0.00	700
Contingency.Cause	65.71	43.40	52.27	46.67	13.21	20.59	5300
Contingency.Cause+ Belief	0.00	0.00	0.00	0.00	0.00	0.00	600
Contingency.Cause+ SpeechAct	0.00	0.00	0.00	0.00	0.00	0.00	200
Contingency. Condition	76.47	81.25	78.79	100	12.50	22.22	1600
Contingency.Purpose	46.15	75.00	57.14	100	12.50	22.22	800
Expansion. Conjunction	65.96	80.17	72.37	76.00	32.76	45.78	11600
Expansion. Disjunction	100	100	100	0.00	0.00	0.00	200
Expansion. Equivalence	0.00	0.00	0.00	0.00	0.00	0.00	600
Expansion. Instantiation	100	33.33	50.00	0.00	0.00	0.00	900
Expansion.Level-of-detail	47.37	62.07	53.73	0.00	0.00	0.00	2900
Expansion.Manner	100	66.67	80.00	100	33.33	50.00	600
Expansion. Substitution	75.00	90.00	81.82	100	10.00	18.18	1000
Hypophora	100	66.67	80.00	0.00	0.00	0.00	600
Temporal. Asynchronous	66.67	63.64	65.12	33.33	4.55	8.00	2200
Temporal. Synchronous	83.33	71.43	76.92	0.00	0.00	0.00	1400
weighted avg	64.93	64.96	62.99	51.38	18.52	25.97	35100
macro avg	62.16	54.52	55.67	36.58	9.81	14.30	35100

[5] In this version of the corpus, 15 documents are missing compared to the original dataset due to pre-processing issues.

	HITS			DiscReT			
eng.rst.gum	P	R	F1	P	R	F1	Num.
adversative	66.67	65.09	65.87	0.00	0.00	0.00	16900
attribution	85.14	89.36	87.20	82.58	90.78	86.49	14100
causal	51.46	54.64	53.00	40.51	32.99	36.36	9700
context	49.80	55.22	52.37	56.83	45.22	50.36	23000
contingency	79.31	92.00	85.19	82.05	64.00	71.91	5000
elaboration	72.05	74.71	73.36	66.00	71.86	68.81	59700
evaluation	46.02	46.43	46.22	44.05	33.04	37.76	11200
explanation	56.38	50.91	53.50	48.06	37.58	42.18	16500
joint	71.03	66.09	68.47	67.26	58.96	62.84	57500
mode	75.47	76.92	76.19	82.61	36.54	50.67	5200
organization	74.59	73.37	73.97	0.00	0.00	0.00	18400
purpose	92.38	89.81	91.08	88.89	51.85	65.50	10800
restatement	60.87	52.83	56.57	63.64	52.83	57.73	5300
topic	71.11	76.19	73.56	60.00	71.43	65.22	4200
weighted avg	68.28	68.19	68.17	55.72	50.33	52.35	257500
macro avg	68.02	68.83	68.32	55.89	46.22	49.70	257500

	HITS			DiscReT			
eng.rst.rstdt	P	R	F1	P	R	F1	Num.
attribution	82.73	97.38	89.46	91.67	97.38	94.44	30500
background	44.44	34.95	39.13	0.00	0.00	0.00	10300
cause	40.00	18.82	25.60	0.00	0.00	0.00	8500
comparison	46.88	53.57	50.00	55.56	17.86	27.03	2800
condition	77.78	74.47	76.09	0.00	0.00	0.00	4700
contrast	61.90	62.33	62.12	0.00	0.00	0.00	14600
elaboration	70.68	79.65	74.90	71.28	67.34	69.25	79600
enablement	68.75	73.33	70.97	90.91	22.22	35.71	4500
evaluation	29.79	17.28	21.88	21.05	9.88	13.45	8100
explanation	33.33	33.64	33.48	27.27	21.82	24.24	11000
joint	64.06	60.43	62.19	56.91	46.52	51.20	23000
manner-means	72.22	48.15	57.78	50.00	3.70	6.90	2700
summary	56.00	43.75	49.12	100	37.50	54.55	3200
temporal	51.79	39.19	44.62	50.00	6.76	11.90	7400
textual-organization	46.15	66.67	54.55	25.00	55.56	34.48	900
topic-change	60.00	23.08	33.33	50.00	7.69	13.33	1300
topic-comment	28.57	16.67	21.05	0.00	0.00	0.00	2400
weighted avg	63.50	65.71	64.02	54.41	46.91	48.78	215500
macro avg	55.00	49.61	50.96	40.57	23.19	25.67	215500

	HITS			DiscReT			
eng.sdrt.stac	P	R	F1	P	R	F1	Num.
Acknowledgement	69.19	58.05	63.13	62.56	59.51	61.00	20500
Alternation	66.67	71.43	68.97	0.00	0.00	0.00	1400
Background	0.00	0.00	0.00	0.00	0.00	0.00	1400
Clarification_question	60.34	60.34	60.34	67.86	65.52	66.67	5800
Comment	54.08	65.70	59.33	50.80	65.70	57.30	24200
Conditional	58.82	66.67	62.50	0.00	0.00	0.00	1500
Continuation	41.98	43.31	42.63	43.81	29.30	35.11	15700
Contrast	48.75	54.93	51.66	0.00	0.00	0.00	7100
Correction	42.42	40.00	41.18	0.00	0.00	0.00	3500
Elaboration	49.18	40.00	44.12	47.22	34.00	39.53	15000
Explanation	38.10	33.33	35.56	25.00	30.56	27.50	7200
Narration	14.29	14.29	14.29	0.00	0.00	0.00	700
Parallel	72.22	72.22	72.22	62.96	47.22	53.97	3600
Q_Elab	52.38	62.26	56.90	55.38	67.92	61.02	5300
Question_answer_pair	88.37	88.89	88.63	0.00	0.00	0.00	34200
Result	38.10	41.03	39.51	0.00	0.00	0.00	3900
weighted avg	60.55	60.79	60.43	33.12	32.52	32.34	151000
macro avg	49.68	50.78	50.06	25.97	24.98	25.13	151000

	HITS			DiscReT			
eus.rst.ert	P	R	F1	P	R	F1	Num.
antithesis	9.09	20.00	12.50	50.00	20.00	28.57	500
background	32.14	31.03	31.58	0.00	0.00	0.00	2900
cause	50.00	35.14	41.27	0.00	0.00	0.00	3700
circumstance	65.22	62.50	63.83	57.14	58.33	57.73	4800
concession	58.82	58.82	58.82	34.78	47.06	40.00	1700
condition	80.00	44.44	57.14	0.00	0.00	0.00	900
conjunction	30.56	44.00	36.07	0.00	0.00	0.00	2500
contrast	35.71	47.62	40.82	0.00	0.00	0.00	2100
disjunction	100	100	100	0.00	0.00	0.00	300
elaboration	53.40	72.86	61.63	48.92	65.00	55.83	14000
evaluation	61.54	50.00	55.17	19.05	25.00	21.62	1600
evidence	66.67	25.00	36.36	0.00	0.00	0.00	800
interpretation	45.45	38.46	41.67	40.00	15.38	22.22	1300
joint	0.00	0.00	0.00	0.00	0.00	0.00	100
justify	16.67	12.50	14.29	33.33	25.00	28.57	800
list	60.98	46.30	52.63	55.56	55.56	55.56	5400
means	63.89	62.16	63.01	58.33	56.76	57.53	3700
motivation	0.00	0.00	0.00	0.00	0.00	0.00	200
preparation	91.07	69.86	79.07	83.87	71.23	77.04	7300
purpose	86.67	78.00	82.11	74.00	74.00	74.00	5000
restatement	55.56	38.46	45.45	57.14	30.77	40.00	1300
result	44.19	55.88	49.35	0.00	0.00	0.00	3400
sequence	56.25	39.13	46.15	43.48	43.48	43.48	2300
solutionhood	20.00	12.50	15.38	14.29	12.50	13.33	800
summary	0.00	0.00	0.00	0.00	0.00	0.00	300
unconditional	0.00	0.00	0.00	0.00	0.00	0.00	100
macro avg	45.53	40.18	41.70	25.77	23.08	23.67	67800
weighted avg	58.30	56.19	56.20	41.83	42.92	41.82	67800

	HITS			DiscReT			
fas.rst.prstc	P	R	F1	P	R	F1	Num.
attribution	60.47	66.67	63.41	61.54	61.54	61.54	3900
background	39.39	41.94	40.62	0.00	0.00	0.00	3100
cause	38.64	48.57	43.04	0.00	0.00	0.00	3500
comparison	66.67	40.00	50.00	0.00	0.00	0.00	500
condition	92.31	80.00	85.71	0.00	0.00	0.00	1500
contrast	58.93	61.11	60.00	0.00	0.00	0.00	5400
elaboration	66.27	73.20	69.57	62.99	63.40	63.19	15300
enablement	60.00	81.82	69.23	88.89	72.73	80.00	1100
evaluation	29.03	36.00	32.14	13.04	12.00	12.50	2500
explanation	38.24	28.89	32.91	20.37	24.44	22.22	4500
joint	61.40	60.34	60.87	43.39	70.69	53.77	11600
manner-means	66.67	28.57	40.00	100	28.57	44.44	700
summary	50.00	31.25	38.46	0.00	0.00	0.00	1600
temporal	55.56	25.00	34.48	100	5.00	9.52	2000
topic-change	0.00	0.00	0.00	0.00	0.00	0.00	900
topic-comment	26.67	36.36	30.77	0.00	0.00	0.00	1100
weighted avg	55.53	56.08	55.22	37.15	38.51	35.47	59200
macro avg	50.64	46.23	46.95	30.64	21.15	21.70	59200

	HITS			DiscReT			
fra.sdrt.annodis	P	R	F1	P	R	F1	Num.
alternation	100	20.00	33.33	0.00	0.00	0.00	500
attribution	76.92	71.43	74.07	47.06	57.14	51.61	1400
background	27.59	19.51	22.86	0.00	0.00	0.00	4100
comment	13.33	15.38	14.29	0.00	0.00	0.00	1300
conditional	100	16.67	28.57	66.67	66.67	66.67	600
continuation	50.00	47.11	48.51	43.66	51.24	47.15	12100
contrast	44.19	65.52	52.78	0.00	0.00	0.00	2900
e-elaboration	59.41	62.50	60.91	53.54	70.83	60.99	9600
elaboration	46.53	52.81	49.47	35.92	41.57	38.54	8900
explanation	53.33	28.57	37.21	29.41	17.86	22.22	2800
explanation*	0.00	0.00	0.00	0.00	0.00	0.00	200
flashback	0.00	0.00	0.00	0.00	0.00	0.00	100
frame	87.76	87.76	87.76	87.80	73.47	80.00	4900
goal	88.24	75.00	81.08	73.68	70.00	71.79	2000
narration	44.09	56.94	49.70	41.18	48.61	44.59	7200
parallel	0.00	0.00	0.00	0.00	0.00	0.00	500
result	40.00	37.50	38.71	0.00	0.00	0.00	3200
temploc	0.00	0.00	0.00	0.00	0.00	0.00	200
weighted avg	52.27	51.84	51.09	38.79	43.04	40.48	62500
macro avg	46.19	36.48	37.74	26.61	27.63	26.86	62500

ita.pdtb.luna	HITS P	HITS R	HITS F1	DiscReT P	DiscReT R	DiscReT F1	Num.
Comparison. Concession	60.00	65.62	62.69	61.54	75.00	67.61	3200
Comparison. Contrast	22.22	18.18	20.00	14.29	9.09	11.11	1100
Contingency.Cause	73.49	71.76	72.62	70.24	69.41	69.82	8500
Contingency. Condition	82.14	69.70	75.41	67.74	63.64	65.62	3300
Contingency.Goal	82.14	88.46	85.19	67.86	73.08	70.37	2600
Expansion	0.00	0.00	0.00	0.00	0.00	0.00	100
Expan- sion.Alternative	100	71.43	83.33	0.00	0.00	0.00	700
Expansion. Conjunction	67.92	61.02	64.29	60.00	45.76	51.92	5900
Expansion. Restatement	54.17	57.78	55.91	0.00	0.00	0.00	4500
Interrupted	100	25.00	40.00	100	50.00	66.67	800
Repetition	68.18	75.00	71.43	0.00	0.00	0.00	2000
Temporal. Asynchronous	53.57	66.67	59.41	52.00	57.78	54.74	4500
Temporal.Synchrony	50.00	37.50	42.86	0.00	0.00	0.00	800
macro avg	62.60	54.47	56.39	37.97	34.14	35.22	38000
weighted avg	66.78	65.00	65.16	49.41	47.63	48.09	38000

nld.rst.nldt	HITS P	HITS R	HITS F1	DiscReT P	DiscReT R	DiscReT F1	Num.
antithesis	0.00	0.00	0.00	0.00	0.00	0.00	200
background	14.29	33.33	20.00	0.00	0.00	0.00	300
circumstance	31.58	37.50	34.29	22.22	12.50	16.00	1600
concession	61.54	66.67	64.00	42.11	66.67	51.61	1200
condition	66.67	75.00	70.59	0.00	0.00	0.00	800
conjunction	37.50	47.37	41.86	0.00	0.00	0.00	1900
contrast	40.00	28.57	33.33	0.00	0.00	0.00	700
disjunction	75.00	75.00	75.00	0.00	0.00	0.00	400
elaboration	70.45	65.26	67.76	61.82	71.58	66.34	9500
enablement	50.00	50.00	50.00	100	25.00	40.00	400
evaluation	40.00	100	57.14	14.29	50.00	22.22	200
evidence	0.00	0.00	0.00	0.00	0.00	0.00	600
interpretation	12.50	10.00	11.11	16.67	10.00	12.50	1000
joint	16.67	33.33	22.22	0.00	0.00	0.00	300
justify	50.00	60.00	54.55	66.67	20.00	30.77	1000
list	33.33	16.67	22.22	37.50	25.00	30.00	1200
means	25.00	25.00	25.00	100	25.00	40.00	400
motivation	69.57	55.17	61.54	43.33	44.83	44.07	2900
nonvolitional-cause	37.50	46.15	41.38	30.77	61.54	41.03	1300
nonvolitional-result	57.14	57.14	57.14	35.71	35.71	35.71	1400
otherwise	0.00	0.00	0.00	0.00	0.00	0.00	100
preparation	55.00	57.89	56.41	36.36	42.11	39.02	1900
purpose	100	83.33	90.91	100	83.33	90.91	600
restatement	0.00	0.00	0.00	0.00	0.00	0.00	200
sequence	57.14	40.00	47.06	33.33	50.00	40.00	1000
solutionhood	50.00	50.00	50.00	0.00	0.00	0.00	800
summary	50.00	25.00	33.33	0.00	0.00	0.00	400
volitional-cause	20.00	50.00	28.57	50.00	50.00	50.00	200
macro avg	40.03	42.44	39.84	28.24	24.05	23.22	32500
weighted avg	53.61	51.69	52.04	39.16	40.62	38.26	32500

por.pdtb.crpc	HITS P	HITS R	HITS F1	DiscReT P	DiscReT R	DiscReT F1	Num.
Comparison	0.00	0.00	0.00	0.00	0.00	0.00	200
Comparison. Concession	80.37	81.90	81.13	74.75	70.48	72.55	10500
Comparison. Contrast	50.00	40.00	44.44	40.00	40.00	40.00	500
Comparison. Similarity	62.50	62.50	62.50	57.14	50.00	53.33	800
Contingency.Cause	72.94	62.63	67.39	60.92	53.54	56.99	9900
Contingency. Condition	68.75	91.67	78.57	83.33	83.33	83.33	1200
Contingency. Negative	0.00	0.00	0.00	0.00	0.00	0.00	100
Contingency.Purpose	86.05	94.87	90.24	88.37	97.44	92.68	3900
Expansion. Conjunction	77.96	83.33	80.56	72.70	81.90	77.03	34800
Expansion. Disjunction	100	100	100	0.00	0.00	0.00	300
Expansion. Equivalence	50.00	28.57	36.36	100	14.29	25.00	700
Expansion.Exception	100	50.00	66.67	0.00	0.00	0.00	600
Expansion. Instantiation	60.00	40.00	48.00	100	20.00	33.33	1500
Expansion.Level	81.56	83.93	82.73	0.00	0.00	0.00	44800
Expansion.Manner	33.33	66.67	44.44	25.00	66.67	36.36	300
Expansion. Substitution	100	60.00	75.00	28.57	40.00	33.33	500
QAP	0.00	0.00	0.00	0.00	0.00	0.00	100
Temporal. Asynchronous	77.19	61.97	68.75	67.74	59.15	63.16	7100
Temporal. Synchronous	73.85	68.57	71.11	0.00	0.00	0.00	7000
macro avg	61.82	56.66	57.78	42.03	35.62	35.11	124800
weighted avg	78.25	78.53	78.14	41.28	41.35	40.66	124800

por.pdtb.tedm	HITS P	HITS R	HITS F1	DiscReT P	DiscReT R	DiscReT F1	Num.
Comparison. Concession	52.27	88.46	65.71	43.14	84.62	57.14	2600
Comparison. Contrast	50.00	5.26	9.52	0.00	0.00	0.00	1900
Comparison. Similarity	33.33	50.00	40.00	33.33	50.00	40.00	200
Contingency.Cause	81.08	61.22	69.77	69.05	59.18	63.74	4900
Contingency.Cause+ Belief	0.00	0.00	0.00	0.00	0.00	0.00	300
Contingency. Condition	80.00	80.00	80.00	90.91	66.67	76.92	1500
Contingency. Condition+ SpeechAct	0.00	0.00	0.00	0.00	0.00	0.00	100
Contingency.Purpose	88.24	100	93.75	100	86.67	92.86	1500
Expansion. Conjunction	67.54	70.64	69.06	59.84	69.72	64.41	10900
Expansion. Disjunction	100	100	100	0.00	0.00	0.00	200
Expansion. Equivalence	0.00	0.00	0.00	0.00	0.00	0.00	300
Expansion. Instantiation	80.00	30.77	44.44	50.00	7.69	13.33	1300
Expansion.Level-of-detail	51.32	75.00	60.94	0.00	0.00	0.00	5200
Expansion.Manner	100	66.67	80.00	50.00	33.33	40.00	300
Expansion. Substitution	20.00	50.00	28.57	50.00	50.00	50.00	200
Hypophora	83.33	71.43	76.92	0.00	0.00	0.00	700
Temporal. Asynchronous	63.64	30.43	41.18	71.43	21.74	33.33	2300
Temporal. Synchronous	73.91	85.00	79.07	0.00	0.00	0.00	2000
weighted avg	65.96	64.84	62.73	45.33	43.68	42.35	36400
macro avg	56.93	53.61	52.16	34.32	29.42	29.54	36400

por.rst.cstn	HITS P	HITS R	HITS F1	DiscReT P	DiscReT R	DiscReT F1	Num.
attribution	100	100	100	100	100	100	1700
background	0.00	0.00	0.00	0.00	0.00	0.00	200
circumstance	75.00	90.00	81.82	66.67	80.00	72.73	1000
comparison	75.00	54.55	63.16	80.00	36.36	50.00	1100
concession	33.33	100	50.00	50.00	100	66.67	100
contrast	50.00	66.67	57.14	0.00	0.00	0.00	300
elaboration	73.33	81.05	77.00	62.70	83.16	71.49	9500
enablement	0.00	0.00	0.00	0.00	0.00	0.00	100
evidence	20.00	33.33	25.00	0.00	0.00	0.00	300
explanation	33.33	10.00	15.38	0.00	0.00	0.00	1000
justify	0.00	0.00	0.00	33.33	16.67	22.22	600
list	68.89	60.78	64.58	57.41	60.78	59.05	5100
means	50.00	100	66.67	100	100	100	100
nonvolitional-cause	16.67	25.00	20.00	0.00	0.00	0.00	400
nonvolitional-result	0.00	0.00	0.00	0.00	0.00	0.00	200
parenthetical	95.83	100	97.87	100	86.96	93.02	2300
purpose	91.67	84.62	88.00	100	61.54	76.19	1300
restatement	0.00	0.00	0.00	0.00	0.00	0.00	100
sequence	37.50	60.00	46.15	50.00	40.00	44.44	1000
volitional-cause	0.00	0.00	0.00	100	33.33	50.00	300
volitional-result	0.00	0.00	0.00	50.00	20.00	28.57	500
macro avg	39.07	46.00	40.61	45.24	38.99	39.73	27200
weighted avg	66.98	68.75	67.19	62.98	64.71	62.31	27200

rus.rst.rrt	HITS P	HITS R	HITS F1	DiscReT P	DiscReT R	DiscReT F1	Num.
antithesis	0.00	0.00	0.00	0.00	0.00	0.00	200
attribution	78.69	82.76	80.67	85.00	87.93	86.44	5800
background	25.86	22.06	23.81	0.00	0.00	0.00	6800
cause	56.34	57.69	57.01	0.00	0.00	0.00	20800
cause-effect	60.00	22.22	32.43	0.00	0.00	0.00	2700
comparison	30.95	31.71	31.33	23.53	19.51	21.33	4100
concession	76.92	74.07	75.47	68.97	74.07	71.43	2700
condition	79.29	77.46	78.36	0.00	0.00	0.00	17300
contrast	68.59	64.85	66.67	0.00	0.00	0.00	20200
effect	0.00	0.00	0.00	0.00	0.00	0.00	100
elaboration	60.36	67.33	63.65	58.69	71.33	64.39	70100
evaluation	48.00	44.44	46.15	48.96	34.81	40.69	13500
evidence	28.57	24.66	26.47	0.00	0.00	0.00	7300
interpretation-evaluation	18.75	20.00	19.35	0.00	0.00	0.00	1500
joint	70.51	67.36	68.90	68.05	68.55	68.30	67100
preparation	40.78	48.99	44.51	55.56	57.05	56.29	14900
purpose	85.37	76.09	80.46	78.72	80.43	79.57	9200
restatement	66.67	66.67	66.67	77.27	70.83	73.91	2400
sequence	60.00	54.00	56.84	56.67	56.67	56.67	15000
solutionhood	8.70	7.69	8.16	4.55	3.85	4.17	2600
macro avg	48.22	45.50	46.35	31.30	31.25	31.16	284300
weighted avg	61.14	60.99	60.87	44.73	47.41	45.86	284300

	HITS			DiscReT			
spa.rst.rststb	P	R	F1	P	R	F1	Num.
antithesis	60.00	56.25	58.06	71.43	62.50	66.67	1600
background	58.33	56.00	57.14	0.00	0.00	0.00	2500
cause	45.45	35.71	40.00	0.00	0.00	0.00	1400
circumstance	58.82	62.50	60.61	69.23	56.25	62.07	1600
concession	70.00	70.00	70.00	70.00	70.00	70.00	1000
condition	100	61.54	76.19	0.00	0.00	0.00	1300
conjunction	0.00	0.00	0.00	0.00	0.00	0.00	300
contrast	72.73	66.67	69.57	0.00	0.00	0.00	1200
elaboration	47.58	66.29	55.40	50.36	77.53	61.06	8900
evaluation	0.00	0.00	0.00	0.00	0.00	0.00	400
evidence	16.67	7.69	10.53	0.00	0.00	0.00	1300
interpretation	50.00	36.36	42.11	14.29	9.09	11.11	1100
joint	44.44	53.33	48.48	43.75	46.67	45.16	1500
justify	60.00	30.00	40.00	0.00	0.00	0.00	1000
list	50.00	35.71	41.67	42.55	35.71	38.83	5600
means	68.18	93.75	78.95	71.43	93.75	81.08	1600
motivation	50.00	33.33	40.00	0.00	0.00	0.00	300
preparation	88.89	85.11	86.96	91.49	91.49	91.49	4700
purpose	100	100	100	100	90.91	95.24	1100
restatement	0.00	0.00	0.00	0.00	0.00	0.00	100
result	48.48	72.73	58.18	0.00	0.00	0.00	2200
sequence	22.22	18.18	20.00	50.00	54.55	52.17	1100
solutionhood	75.00	50.00	60.00	0.00	0.00	0.00	600
summary	0.00	0.00	0.00	0.00	0.00	0.00	100
unless	0.00	0.00	0.00	0.00	0.00	0.00	100
macro avg	47.47	43.65	44.55	26.98	27.54	27.00	42600
weighted avg	56.85	57.28	55.95	41.60	46.24	43.16	42600

	HITS			DiscReT			
spa.rst.sctb	P	R	F1	P	R	F1	Num.
antithesis	0.00	0.00	0.00	0.00	0.00	0.00	300
background	28.57	50.00	36.36	0.00	0.00	0.00	400
circumstance	20.00	33.33	25.00	50.00	33.33	40.00	300
condition	100	100	100	0.00	0.00	0.00	100
conjunction	0.00	0.00	0.00	0.00	0.00	0.00	100
contrast	80.00	80.00	80.00	0.00	0.00	0.00	500
disjunction	100	50.00	66.67	0.00	0.00	0.00	200
elaboration	83.33	56.34	67.23	77.19	61.97	68.75	7100
enablement	0.00	0.00	0.00	0.00	0.00	0.00	100
evidence	0.00	0.00	0.00	0.00	0.00	0.00	100
interpretation	66.67	66.67	66.67	100	33.33	50.00	300
list	78.12	75.76	76.92	69.44	75.76	72.46	3300
means	50.00	100	66.67	50.00	100	66.67	200
motivation	0.00	0.00	0.00	0.00	0.00	0.00	100
preparation	47.62	100	64.52	64.29	90.00	75.00	1000
purpose	100	85.71	92.31	85.71	85.71	85.71	700
result	60.00	60.00	60.00	0.00	0.00	0.00	500
sequence	25.00	20.00	22.22	37.50	60.00	46.15	500
summary	0.00	0.00	0.00	0.00	0.00	0.00	100
macro avg	44.17	46.20	43.40	28.11	28.43	26.57	15900
weighted avg	70.88	61.64	64.16	61.34	57.23	58.22	15900

	HITS			DiscReT			
tha.pdtb.tdtb	P	R	F1	P	R	F1	Num.
Comparison.Concession	93.88	93.24	93.56	92.95	97.97	95.39	14800
Comparison.Contrast	83.33	86.21	84.75	87.21	86.21	86.71	8700
Comparison.Similarity	100	100	100	100	100	100	100
Contingency.Cause	98.09	99.23	98.66	95.13	98.07	96.58	25900
Contingency.Cause+Belief	0.00	0.00	0.00	0.00	0.00	0.00	300
Contingency.Condition	93.41	91.40	92.39	92.31	90.32	91.30	9300
Contingency.Condition+SpeechAct	0.00	0.00	0.00	0.00	0.00	0.00	100
Contingency.Negative-Condition	0.00	0.00	0.00	0.00	0.00	0.00	300
Contingency.Purpose	100	100	100	100	97.80	98.89	9100
Expansion.Conjunction	99.61	97.69	98.64	96.15	96.15	96.15	26000
Expansion.Disjunction	100	100	100	0.00	0.00	0.00	2800
Expansion.Exception	100	100	100	0.00	0.00	0.00	200
Expansion.GenExpansion	99.52	100	99.76	0.00	0.00	0.00	20600
Expansion.Instantiation	100	100	100	100	100	100	100
Expansion.Level-of-detail	0.00	0.00	0.00	0.00	0.00	0.00	100
Expansion.Substitution	66.67	100	80.00	0.00	0.00	0.00	200
Temporal.Asynchronous	93.10	95.07	94.08	93.15	95.77	94.44	14200
Temporal.Synchronous	65.00	81.25	72.22	0.00	0.00	0.00	1600
macro avg	71.81	74.67	73.00	47.61	47.91	47.75	134400
weighted avg	95.48	95.83	95.64	75.96	77.01	76.47	134400

	HITS			DiscReT			
tur.pdtb.tdb	P	R	F1	P	R	F1	Num.
Comparison.Concession	53.66	66.67	59.46	59.26	48.48	53.33	3300
Comparison.Concession+SpeechAct	0.00	0.00	0.00	0.00	0.00	0.00	200
Comparison.Contrast	71.43	23.81	35.71	41.67	23.81	30.30	2100
Comparison.Similarity	66.67	66.67	66.67	50.00	33.33	40.00	300
Contingency.Cause	44.83	30.23	36.11	32.31	48.84	38.89	4300
Contingency.Cause+Belief	0.00	0.00	0.00	0.00	0.00	0.00	400
Contingency.Cause+SpeechAct	0.00	0.00	0.00	0.00	0.00	0.00	300
Contingency.Condition	50.00	45.45	47.62	50.00	27.27	35.29	1100
Contingency.Negative-condition	0.00	0.00	0.00	0.00	0.00	0.00	200
Contingency.Purpose	90.00	75.00	81.82	88.89	66.67	76.19	1200
Expansion.Conjunction	51.06	66.06	57.60	44.77	70.64	54.80	10900
Expansion.Correction	0.00	0.00	0.00	0.00	0.00	0.00	200
Expansion.Disjunction	60.00	100	75.00	0.00	0.00	0.00	300
Expansion.Equivalence	50.00	20.00	28.57	0.00	0.00	0.00	500
Expansion.Exception	0.00	0.00	0.00	0.00	0.00	0.00	100
Expansion.Instantiation	20.00	12.50	15.38	100	12.50	22.22	800
Expansion.Level-of-detail	0.00	0.00	0.00	0.00	0.00	0.00	4500
Expansion.Manner	50.00	25.00	33.33	40.00	33.33	36.36	1200
Expansion.Substitution	0.00	0.00	0.00	0.00	0.00	0.00	200
Hypophora	0.00	0.00	0.00	0.00	0.00	0.00	300
Temporal.Asynchronous	72.34	57.63	64.15	70.97	37.29	48.89	5900
Temporal.Synchronous	52.38	56.41	54.32	0.00	0.00	0.00	3900
macro avg	33.29	29.34	29.81	26.27	18.28	19.83	42200
weighted avg	47.62	45.50	45.13	38.70	37.44	35.46	42200

	HITS			DiscReT			
tur.pdtb.tedm	P	R	F1	P	R	F1	Num.
Comparison.Concession	56.10	88.46	68.66	47.50	73.08	57.58	2600
Comparison.Concession+SpeechAct	0.00	0.00	0.00	0.00	0.00	0.00	100
Comparison.Contrast	66.67	16.67	26.67	40.00	50.00	44.44	1200
Comparison.Similarity	100	37.50	54.55	50.00	25.00	33.33	800
Contingency.Cause	48.94	46.00	47.42	52.27	46.00	48.94	5000
Contingency.Cause+Belief	0.00	0.00	0.00	0.00	0.00	0.00	600
Contingency.Cause+SpeechAct	0.00	0.00	0.00	0.00	0.00	0.00	100
Contingency.Condition	62.50	78.95	69.77	68.75	57.89	62.86	1900
Contingency.Negative-condition	0.00	0.00	0.00	0.00	0.00	0.00	100
Contingency.Purpose	88.24	71.43	78.95	94.44	80.95	87.18	2100
Expansion	0.00	0.00	0.00	0.00	0.00	0.00	100
Expansion.Conjunction	50.89	61.96	55.88	43.61	63.04	51.56	9200
Expansion.Disjunction	100	100	100	0.00	0.00	0.00	500
Expansion.Equivalence	66.67	28.57	40.00	0.00	0.00	0.00	700
Expansion.Exception	0.00	0.00	0.00	0.00	0.00	0.00	200
Expansion.Instantiation	25.00	9.09	13.33	66.67	18.18	28.57	1100
Expansion.Level-of-detail	37.25	50.00	42.70	0.00	0.00	0.00	3800
Expansion.Manner	0.00	0.00	0.00	60.00	42.86	50.00	700
Expansion.Substitution	88.89	72.73	80.00	60.00	54.55	57.14	1100
Hypophora	75.00	42.86	54.55	0.00	0.00	0.00	700
Temporal.Asynchronous	53.33	40.00	45.71	20.00	15.00	17.14	2000
Temporal.Synchronous	56.52	72.22	63.41	0.00	0.00	0.00	1800
macro avg	44.36	37.11	38.25	27.42	23.93	24.49	36400
weighted avg	53.49	54.12	51.93	39.13	41.21	38.87	36400

	HITS			DiscReT			
zho.dep.scidtb	P	R	F1	P	R	F1	Num.
attribution	92.31	100	96.00	90.91	83.33	86.96	1200
bg-compare	0.00	0.00	0.00	0.00	0.00	0.00	300
bg-general	62.07	75.00	67.92	65.38	70.83	68.00	2400
bg-goal	0.00	0.00	0.00	0.00	0.00	0.00	400
comparison	66.67	100	80.00	66.67	100	80.00	200
condition	0.00	0.00	0.00	0.00	0.00	0.00	100
contrast	50.00	57.14	53.33	0.00	0.00	0.00	700
elab-addition	65.75	66.67	66.21	61.18	72.22	66.24	7200
elab-process_step	50.00	66.67	57.14	100	16.67	28.57	600
enablement	77.27	73.91	75.56	70.83	73.91	72.34	2300
evaluation	90.91	76.92	83.33	78.57	84.62	81.48	1300
exp-reason	0.00	0.00	0.00	0.00	0.00	0.00	100
joint	69.44	78.12	73.53	67.65	71.88	69.70	3200
manner-means	33.33	25.00	28.57	50.00	25.00	33.33	400
progression	0.00	0.00	0.00	0.00	0.00	0.00	400
result	75.00	50.00	60.00	0.00	0.00	0.00	600
temporal	50.00	100	66.67	0.00	0.00	0.00	100
macro avg	46.04	51.14	47.54	38.31	35.20	34.51	21500
weighted avg	64.79	67.44	65.77	59.60	62.33	59.83	21500

	HITS			DiscReT			
zho.pdtb.cdtb	P	R	F1	P	R	F1	Num.
Alternative	0.00	0.00	0.00	0.00	0.00	0.00	100
Causation	0.00	0.00	0.00	0.00	0.00	0.00	5300
Conditional	0.00	0.00	0.00	0.00	0.00	0.00	2200
Conjunction	59.52	100	74.63	0.00	0.00	0.00	45000
Contrast	0.00	0.00	0.00	0.00	0.00	0.00	4600
Expansion	100	1.64	3.23	0.00	0.00	0.00	12200
Progression	0.00	0.00	0.00	0.00	0.00	0.00	900
Purpose	0.00	0.00	0.00	87.50	50.00	63.64	1400
Temporal	0.00	0.00	0.00	77.50	75.61	76.54	4100
weighted avg	51.43	59.63	44.82	5.81	5.01	5.32	75800
macro avg	17.72	11.29	8.65	18.33	13.96	15.58	75800

	HITS			DiscReT			
zho.rst.gcdt	P	R	F1	P	R	F1	Num.
adversative-antithesis	50.00	25.00	33.33	0.00	0.00	0.00	800
adversative-concession	47.06	57.14	51.61	48.78	71.43	57.97	2800
adversative-contrast	48.57	58.62	53.12	39.47	51.72	44.78	2900
attribution-negative	100	100	100	100	100	100	100
attribution-positive	93.02	93.02	93.02	83.67	95.35	89.13	4300
causal-cause	51.85	37.84	43.75	44.74	45.95	45.33	3700
causal-result	12.50	9.09	10.53	14.29	4.55	6.90	2200
context-background	30.77	44.44	36.36	38.46	41.67	40.00	3600
context-circumstance	91.18	73.81	81.58	83.87	61.90	71.23	4200
contingency-condition	90.48	65.52	76.00	80.95	58.62	68.00	2900
elaboration-additional	27.55	49.09	35.29	22.95	25.45	24.14	5500
elaboration-attribute	91.51	79.51	85.09	94.39	82.79	88.21	12200
evaluation-comment	23.53	36.36	28.57	30.77	36.36	33.33	1100
explanation-evidence	41.18	36.84	38.89	0.00	0.00	0.00	3800
explanation-justify	11.54	14.29	12.77	0.00	0.00	0.00	2100
explanation-motivation	0.00	0.00	0.00	0.00	0.00	0.00	800
joint-disjunction	0.00	0.00	0.00	50.00	33.33	40.00	300
joint-list	63.82	65.13	64.47	0.00	0.00	0.00	19500
joint-other	13.16	15.62	14.29	25.00	15.62	19.23	3200
joint-sequence	71.05	44.26	54.55	0.00	0.00	0.00	6100
mode-manner	66.67	33.33	44.44	33.33	16.67	22.22	600
mode-means	50.00	53.85	51.85	45.45	38.46	41.67	1300
organization-heading	86.21	73.53	79.37	73.33	64.71	68.75	3400
organization-phatic	0.00	0.00	0.00	0.00	0.00	0.00	100
organization-preparation	58.33	58.33	58.33	75.76	69.44	72.46	3600
purpose-attribute	0.00	0.00	0.00	0.00	0.00	0.00	200
purpose-goal	56.00	56.00	56.00	0.00	0.00	0.00	2500
restatement-partial	7.69	11.11	9.09	13.33	22.22	16.67	900
restatement-repetition	0.00	0.00	0.00	0.00	0.00	0.00	100
topic-question	83.33	100	90.91	55.56	100	71.43	500
weighted avg	59.70	56.35	57.25	37.68	35.47	36.10	95300
macro avg	45.57	43.06	43.44	35.14	34.54	34.05	95300

	HITS			DiscReT			
zho.rst.sctb	P	R	F1	P	R	F1	Num.
antithesis	50.00	33.33	40.00	0.00	0.00	0.00	300
background	100	25.00	40.00	0.00	0.00	0.00	400
circumstance	66.67	50.00	57.14	0.00	0.00	0.00	400
condition	100	100	100	0.00	0.00	0.00	100
conjunction	0.00	0.00	0.00	0.00	0.00	0.00	200
contrast	100	20.00	33.33	0.00	0.00	0.00	500
disjunction	100	50.00	66.67	0.00	0.00	0.00	200
elaboration	78.18	62.32	69.35	68.97	57.97	62.99	6900
enablement	0.00	0.00	0.00	0.00	0.00	0.00	100
evidence	100	100	100	0.00	0.00	0.00	100
interpretation	25.00	33.33	28.57	0.00	0.00	0.00	300
list	62.50	78.12	69.44	55.56	62.50	58.82	3200
means	33.33	50.00	40.00	0.00	0.00	0.00	200
motivation	0.00	0.00	0.00	0.00	0.00	0.00	100
preparation	50.00	100	66.67	66.67	83.33	74.07	1200
purpose	50.00	33.33	40.00	20.00	16.67	18.18	600
restatement	0.00	0.00	0.00	0.00	0.00	0.00	100
result	28.57	50.00	36.36	0.00	0.00	0.00	400
sequence	33.33	40.00	36.36	33.33	20.00	25.00	500
summary	0.00	0.00	0.00	0.00	0.00	0.00	100
macro avg	48.88	41.27	41.20	12.23	12.02	11.95	15900
weighted avg	65.62	60.38	60.06	47.94	45.28	46.24	15900

DiscoFlan: Instruction Fine-tuning and Refined Text Generation for Discourse Relation Label Classification

Kaveri Anuranjana
Language Science and Technology
Saarland University
kaveri@coli.uni-saarland.de

Abstract

This paper introduces DiscoFlan, our system for the DISRPT 2023 shared task on discourse relation classification. We leverage recent advances in NLP finetuning and use Flan-T5 as a multilingual discourse relation classifier. Our model uses multilingual instructional prompts to finetune on datasets from different languages and generate relation labels as classification outputs. The model's hyperparameters are tuned to enable efficient label generation by finetuning on low-resource datasets. Moreover, we introduce a post-processing step to tackle the problem of label mismatches caused by the generative nature of a seq2seq model by using the label distribution. In contrast to the previous state-of-the-art model, our approach eliminates the need for hand-crafted features in computing the discourse relation classes. Overall, DiscoFlan showcases how instruction finetuning can perform multilingual discourse relation classification for the DISRPT 2023 discourse relation classification shared task.

1 Introduction

Discourse Relation Classification (DRC) is a discourse-level task that requires the identification of discourse relations between text segments in a document. This low-resourced task contains multiple subtasks with different languages and formalisms. The numbers of unique labels vary from 9 in zho.pdtb.cdtb to 33 in nld.rst.nldt.

We train DiscoFlan and compare it with the current state-of-the-art model as well as a multilingual classification baseline on the DISRPT datasets and present our results for the 2023 DISRPT sharedtask for Discourse Relation Classification.

Supervised Large language models (LLMs) trained with human labels are truly a paradigm shift due to their zero-shot and low-resource capabilities. Improved language representation mechanisms and utilization of large pre-training corpora of LLMs have led to significant advancements in two key areas: zero-shot capabilities and low-resource prompt learning. In this paper, we focus on low-resource DRC. Such breakthroughs are a testament to the power of large-scale pretraining. With enhanced representations, language models can generalize and transfer knowledge across different tasks and domains, enabling impressive zero-shot capabilities where models can perform well on tasks they were not explicitly trained on. These improved zero-shot learners have the capability to learn efficiently on low-resource complex tasks like Relation Classification. The availability of even limited amounts of training data allows for effective low-resource prompt learning. These advancements highlight the immense potential of LLMs and their ability to tackle the real-world problem of DRC.

Our main contributions are: **1.** We perform instruction finetuning of multilingual prompts with DiscoFlan for DRC tasks of different formalisms and languages to develop a seq2seq generative label classification system. **2.** We use a simple post-processing stage harnessing the label distributions using majority label distributions for low resource dataset.[1]

2 Related Work

2.1 Instruction Finetuning

LLMs, such as InstructGPT (Ouyang et al., 2022), ChatGPT, FLAN-T5-XXL(13B) (Chung et al., 2022), LLaMA (Touvron et al., 2023) have revolutionized natural language processing. Fine-tuning, a process of training these models on specific tasks enhances their performance and is typically used for low-resource classification where creating large annotated datasets can be difficult resulting in small dataset sizes. Instruction fine-tuning leverages the models' powerful representations and contextual

[1]We release our code here: https://github.com/erzaliator/DiscoFlan

Proceedings of the 3rd Shared Task on Discourse Relation Parsing and Treebanking (DISRPT 2023), pages 22–28
July 14, 2023

understanding to achieve superior accuracy and efficiency in a wide range of NLP tasks. This approach enables adaptation of large language models to suit specific applications, making them valuable tools for natural language understanding and generation.

FlanT5 (Chung et al., 2022) is a generative LLM that has gained significant attention in the field of natural language processing (NLP). It is based on the T5 (Text-To-Text Transfer Transformer) architecture (Kale and Rastogi, 2020) and is pre-trained on a massive corpus of text data. FlanT5, demonstrates strong multi task generalization capabilities through the training paradigm of instruction finetuning, a process that involves further training the base model on specific NLP tasks with task-specific data and instructions. By providing explicit instructions during the finetuning phase, the model's underlying representations and contextual understanding can be harnessed to achieve superior performance in various NLP applications.

Motivated by the strong NLU capabilities of FlanT5 (Chung et al., 2022), similarly, we finetune FlanT5 to learn discourse relation classification by posing it as a seq2seq generative task. For the respective DISRPT discourse relation datasets, the model is tasked with generating sequences that correspond to the discourse relations from that dataset. We perform instruction finetuning on each individual dataset by using a suitable prompt template to the sentence pairs to harness the structured prompt input format that FlanT5 is pre-trained on for multi-task reasoning.

Language	Prompt
Chinese	"sent1 和 sent2 之间的话语关系是什么： sent1: 该公司报告了 2023 年第三季度的最高利润 sent2: 近期公司市值的增加对市场情绪产生了积极影响。"
English	"what discourse relation holds between sent1 and sent2: sent1: The company is reporting the highest profits for Q3 2023. sent2: The recent increase in the company's market cap has impacted market sentiments positively.
Italian	"Quale relazione discorsiva c'è tra sent1 e sent2: sent1: La società sta riportando i profitti più alti per il terzo trimestre del 2023. sent2: Il recente aumento della capitalizzazione di mercato della società ha avuto un impatto positivo sui sentimenti di mercato.

Figure 1: Prompt template for DRC in different languages for instruction finetuning. We translate the prompt across datasets.

2.2 Multilingual Discourse Classification

Discourse relations refer to the connections and dependencies between different parts of a text that contribute to its overall coherence and meaning. Various annotation frameworks have been proposed for the task of DRC such as RST(Carlson et al., 2002), PDTB(Prasad et al., 2008) and SDRT(Lascarides and Asher, 2007) among others. The Discourse Relation Parsing and Treebanking (DISRPT) provides DRC datasets across various languages and formalisms in the form of a sentence pair classification task (Zeldes et al., 2021).

Kurfalı and Östling (2019) applied cross-lingual transfer learning on the DRC task but only evaluated in a zero-shot setting. Their results were considerably below the state-of-the-art system. DiscoDisco (Gessler et al., 2021) obtains the state-of-the-art performance by using hand-crafted features to descibe the discourse segments and training with individual checkpoints for each language.

3 Methodology

3.1 Modelling Classification as a Refined Label Generation task

With instruction finetuning, the model learns to generate discourse labels given a prompt encoding the input sentence pair. The decoded output is passed through a refinement stage which ensures that mismatches are removed based on the dataset label distribution.

3.1.1 Generating labels using seq2seq model

Classification is typically performed using AutoEncoder models which are pre-trained on data-denoising objectives such as Mask Language Modelling. These models are finetuned for classification with a final prediction layer (Jin et al., 2020) to learn label representations from the model's hidden representations. FlanT5 (Chung et al., 2022) is an EncoderDecoder model which was trained with Instruction Finetuning objective. On the other hand, current-state-of-the-art Discourse Relation Classifiers are AutoEncoder based architectures (Gessler et al., 2021; Jiang et al., 2022) which use a prediction layer to encode the labels as discrete categories.

Instruction-based prompts: The input is formulated as an instruction-based prompt to utilize the Instruction Finetuning capabilities of FlanT5. It is modified as shown in Figure 1.

DiscoFlan: The FlanT5 decoder is adopted to generate discourse relation labels. The model is called DiscoFlan as the decoder hyperparameters are adjusted to generate short sequenced labels and the model is finetuned on DRC datasets.

Finetuning: The model is trained with standard loss for training EncoderDecoder models. During training, through a conditional generation cross entropy loss meant for sequence generation, the model learns to generate a sequence corresponding to the relation label rather than a typical classification cross entropy loss used to learn categorical representations.

Generating Discourse Relation labels: During inference, the decoder's output tokens are used for generating discourse relation labels. This has the added benefit of utilizing the task representations of the FlanT5 to generate sequences grounded in real-world knowledge to incorporate label meaning. This grounds the meaning of the relation labels to the model's generative space which is significantly richer than using one-hot representations. (Yung et al., 2022) also note that using one-hot encoding for label representation ignores the inherent ambiguity of discourse relation labels.

We can investigate the effect of using special numeric tokens for classification, however, we leave that to future work.

3.1.2 Refinement logic

While working with discourse relation classifiers it is empirically observed that relation classification models are prone to a large number of false predictions of the majority label. Additionally, due to a lack of training data which is generally the case for DRC datasets, DiscoFlan generates substantial mismatches. These mismatches can be partial or complete. In order to alleviate the issue of mismatches and to construct a system submission for the shared task we propose a processing step after the label generation stage. This allows the model's generated outputs to be refined to suit the shared task's analysis criterion i.e. the outputs always belong to the set of dataset labels.

Mismatches are strings that do not belong to the label space. For example - The RST label *elaboration* being incorrectly generated as *elab* by the model. While developing DiscoFlan it was observed that a significant portion of the mismatches were of the form - *elaboration of, elaborated, elaborating*. Hence, a simple post-processing stage is used to refine the decoder's generated sequences during evaluation. After removing the noisy affixes (such as *"-er", "-ed"*, etc.), the remaining lemma is matched against the training set's labels (for out-of-domain datasets, the validation set labels are used). The label matching with the lemma is used as the final output.

When the prediction lemma does not belong to the label space, it is replaced with the majority label of the training dataset. Figure 2 provides such an example.

This modification is denoted as **DiscoFlan+Ref**.

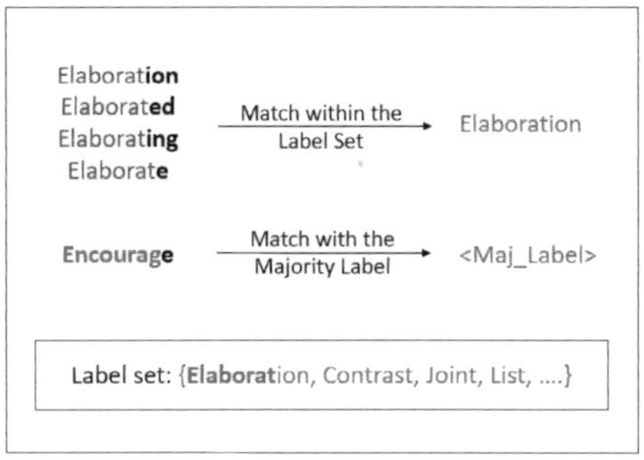

Figure 2: Refinement stage for the decoded output implemented for DiscoFlan+Ref.

3.2 Baseline (Xlm-R classifier)

DiscoFlan is a multilingual model whereas previous models for DRC have been monolingual with separate language models for each dataset. In order to assess the impact of using multilingual representations, we also compare our results with **Xlm-R** (Conneau et al., 2020) model for multilingual representations which has been shown to perform well on NLI tasks across a diverse set of languages.

3.2.1 Training Setup

The performances of DiscoFlan and other variants are assessed for Discourse Relation Classification using the weights provided by HuggingFace library [2]. Due to practical considerations, FlanT5-small is used (specifically, google/flan-t5-small is used as the model type). The FlanT5-small model consists of significantly lesser parameters as compared to FlanT5-base.

For comparability, the same hyperparameters are kept for all models across all language pairs. A batch size of 16 is used for all runs. The models are trained for 50 epochs with an Early Stopping patience of 12 calls. 5 or 10 epochs are used to

[2] `https://huggingface.co/docs/transformers/model_doc/flan-t5`

train the larger datasets. Details of the epoch hyperparameter can be found in our code. The smaller datasets are trained with a high learning rate, $1e-3$ while the larger datasets use a smaller learning rate of $1e-5$.

The huggingface Transformer and Pytorch library are used. Each instance of a model is run on a 32 GB Nvidia Tesla V100 GPU card.

3.2.2 Model Setup

It is noted that raw generations are sensitive to the model parameters - max generation length, min generation length. Figure 4 shows the average label length for the datasets. The average length varies from 8 to 22 characters within the shared task.

The minimum generation length and maximum generation length are set on a per-dataset basis. Readers are suggested to refer to our code to obtain these values for each dataset.

Reducing the beam width improves the quality of generations. A smaller beam width means that the model only considers a limited number of candidates at each decoding step. When generating small text, such as labels for classification tasks, small beam width is suitable. Additionally, smaller beam width leads to faster model convergence as the generation will favour a specific set of candidates early on. A beam width of 4 is used.

4 Results

4.1 Learning seq2seq representations

We train DiscoFlan on the DISRPT datasets and present our results for the 2023 DISRPT sharedtask for Discourse Relation Classification. Firstly, we make predictions using raw generated tokens. The results are presented in Table 1 (column DiscoFlan). Secondly, we apply simple refinement logic to exploit the distribution of discourse labels. The results are also presented in Table 1 (column DiscoFlan+Ref).

5 Analysis

5.1 Refinement improves low resource relation classification

Table 1 shows how the refinement logic helps the model to infer better labels. We find that supervision alone is not enough to produce good labels. Many of the labels that the model generates are not in the label space. We fix this by replacing them with the most common label prediction. This improves the model performance for all the datasets. The 2023 DISRPT sharedtask adds 11 more datasets to the 15 datasets that the previous best models used. DiscoFlan+Ref does not use hand crafted features, but it is close to the best model for fas.rst.rpstc. We note that the model often overfits on one label. This means that we need to improve the instruction fine-tuning, because just using the text and a suitable loss function is not sufficient.

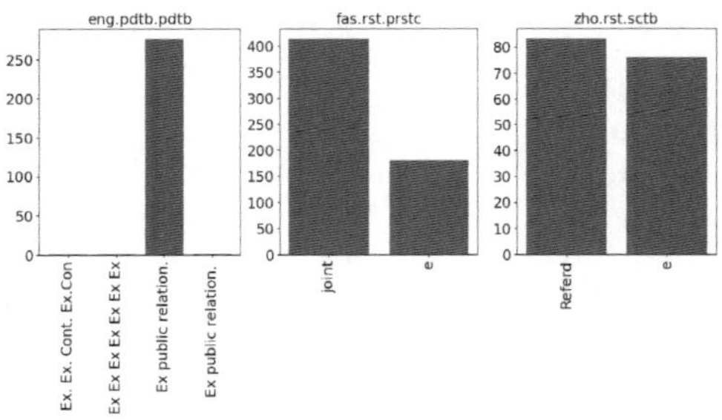

Figure 3: Labels predicted by DiscoFlan for datasets eng.pdtb.pdtb, fas.rst.prstc, zho.rst.sctb

Additionally, **DiscoFlan+Ref** outperforms the **DiscoFlan** model for low-resource datasets as it resolves mismatches. This is due to the fact that language generation requires a large amount of data for finetuning. Mismatches are also subsequently higher for generative models. Refinement addresses the issue of complete and partial mismatching caused to generation issues.

This highlights that weak label learners can be augmented with simple distributional logic to improve model classification. The column "Probs" denotes the accuracy achieved by always predicting the majority label. This chance probability bounds the gains that can achieved by **DiscoFlan+Ref**.

Figure 3 shows the labels produced for three sample dataset for **DiscoFlan**. In the case for complex labels like eng.pdtb.pdtb, the model is prone to generating out-of-vocabulary labels. Where the labels are not significantly complex, the model learns to overfit on a single label.

Note that Xlm-R and DiscoDisco [3] are also prone to majority label generation.

6 Conclusion and Future Work

In conclusion, our paper introduces DiscoFlan, a multilingual discourse relation classifier submitted for the DISRPT 2023 shared task. We addressed

[3]The numbers for DiscoDisco reported in Table 1 are taken from the paper

Corpus	DD w/ feats.	DD w/o feats.	DiscoFlan	DiscoFlan+Ref	Baseline	Probs
deu.rst.pcc	39.23	33.85	0.00	13.08	15.51	9.70
eng.dep.covdtb	na	na	0.00	50.15	na	50.25*
eng.dep.scidtb	na	na	0.00	34.12	na	34.59
eng.pdtb.pdtb	74.44	75.63	0.00	24.41	66.95	27.92
eng.pdtb.tedm	na	na	0.00	33.05	na	29.6*
eng.rst.gum	66.76	62.65	0.00	25.39	53.07	21.86
eng.rst.rstdt	67.1	66.45	0.00	36.94	62.47	40.33
eng.sdrt.stac	65.03	59.67	0.00	22.65	43.4	23.74
eus.rst.ert	60.62	59.59	7.96	28.61	22.74	21.4
fas.rst.prstc	52.53	51.18	19.59	45.44	34.01	23.78
fra.sdrt.annodis	46.4	48.32	19.36	19.36	33.12	20.50
ita.pdtb.luna	na	na	0.00	22.37	na	22.3
nld.rst.nldt	55.21	52.15	0.00	35.08	33.84	26.43
por.pdtb.crpc	na	na	7.93	43.83	na	32.1
por.pdtb.tedm	na	na	0.00	29.95	na	25.1*
por.rst.cstn	64.34	67.28	0.36	35.29	58.7	27.74
rus.rst.rrt	66.44	65.46	0.00	23.60	58.05	23.53
spa.rst.rststb	54.23	54.23	5.86	26.76	31.53	20.17
spa.rst.sctb	66.04	61.01	0.00	44.65	46.12	34.16
tha.pdtb.tdtb	na	na	0.00	19.35	na	23.03
tur.pdtb.tdb	60.09	57.58	36.49	36.49	35.23	25.05
tur.pdtb.tedm	na	na	35.71	35.71	na	27.10*
zho.dep.scidtb	na	na	29.00	33.49	48.72	30.92
zho.rst.gcdt	na	na	59.36	59.37	na	18.93
zho.rst.sctb	64.15	64.15	0.00	20.46	47.92	33.25
zho.pdtb.cdtb	86.49	87.34	0.00	43.40	na	66.01

Table 1: Comparing results of Relation Classification results against Xlm-R baseline and state-of-the-art DisCoDisCo (DD) Gessler et al. (2021) in terms of accuracy. We report the accuracy from the DISRPT 2023 sharedtask for DiscoFlan+Ref. Using the released test set and metric, we also report the accuracy for DiscoFlan. Improved numbers are denoted in bold. Accuracy of the current year's new shared task datasets are underlined where model outperforms chance probability.

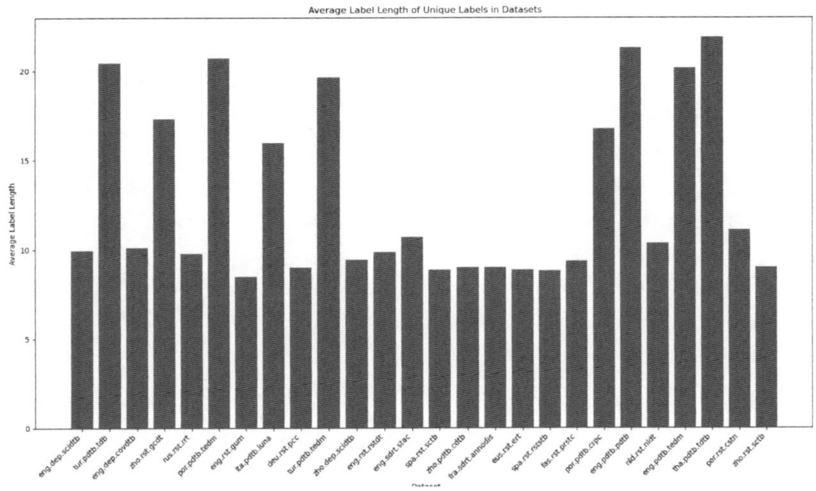

Figure 4: Average unique Label sequence length

the challenge of mismatched in seq2seq models by leveraging label distribution information for label generation.

Our approach eliminates the need for handcrafted features and introduces a novel label generation mechanism that anchors the labels to a fixed set. Emperical results demostrate promising results for DiscoFlan+Ref as well as DiscoFlan compared to the state-of-the-art model and a multilingual baseline.

We analyzed the limitations of multilingual models as weak learners and showed that larger models with richer pre-training objectives, in the form of instruction fine-tuning, yield more meaningful representations.

Post-processing refinement logic improves low-resource relation classification, as evidenced by the consistent outperformance of DiscoFlan+Ref over the baseline model. It addresses issues of mismatches caused by generation problems, leading to enhanced classification accuracy. Our findings highlight the potential of augmenting weak label learners with distributional logic to improve model classification. DiscoFlan showcases instruction finetuning for multilingual discourse relation classification for the DISRPT 2023 shared task and provides valuable insights for future research in this area.

We recognize the potential of larger models to improve prediction quality; however, due to constraints in terms of resources and time, we were unable to test the performance of Flan-T5-Large in our study. Furthermore, we acknowledge that further advancements in decoding strategies and imporved prompts have the potential to enhance label representations and generation. In our future work, we intend to explore these topics to enhance our current models.

Limitations

While using the majority label solves the problem of handing out-of-vocabulary labels during fine-tuning, we acknowledge that label refinement method relies on the majority label. This makes a strong assumption about our dataset bias, namely, that the majority label outnumbers the rest of the labels significantly to impact accuracy. Hence, this method may not be applicable to well-balanced datasets.

We also note that simply predicting the majority label is simple method of label prediction which does not generalized to new unseen datasets. Improving label prediction by enriching datasets manually or automatically might make the task more representative of natural data.

Using larger models can improve model prediction however due to time and machine constraints we leave the evaluation using FlanT5-large for future work.

Ethics Statement

We note that low resource classifiers are prone to overfitting. We encourage users to thoroughly analyse the predicted labels before using our provided models. No other ethical considerations need to be made regarding the data and models.

Acknowledgements

This work is supported by the German Research Foundation (DFG) under Grant SFB 1102 ("Information Density and Linguistic Encoding", Project-ID 232722074). We thank Prof. Vera Demberg, Amir Zeldes, Chloe Braud and Laura Riviere for their valuable time and suggestions in improving our submission. We also thank the DISRPT 2023 organisers for their assistance and feedback on our system submission.

References

Lynn Carlson, Mary Ellen Okurowski, and Daniel Marcu. 2002. *RST discourse treebank*. Linguistic Data Consortium, University of Pennsylvania.

Hyung Won Chung, Le Hou, Shayne Longpre, Barret Zoph, Yi Tay, William Fedus, Eric Li, Xuezhi Wang, Mostafa Dehghani, Siddhartha Brahma, et al. 2022. Scaling instruction-finetuned language models. *arXiv preprint arXiv:2210.11416*.

Alexis Conneau, Kartikay Khandelwal, Naman Goyal, Vishrav Chaudhary, Guillaume Wenzek, Francisco Guzmán, Edouard Grave, Myle Ott, Luke Zettlemoyer, and Veselin Stoyanov. 2020. Unsupervised cross-lingual representation learning at scale. In *Proceedings of the 58th Annual Meeting of the Association for Computational Linguistics*, pages 8440–8451, Online. Association for Computational Linguistics.

Luke Gessler, Shabnam Behzad, Yang Janet Liu, Siyao Peng, Yilun Zhu, and Amir Zeldes. 2021. DisCoDisCo at the DISRPT2021 shared task: A system for discourse segmentation, classification, and connective detection. In *Proceedings of the 2nd Shared Task on Discourse Relation Parsing and Treebanking (DISRPT 2021)*, pages 51–62, Punta Cana, Dominican Republic. Association for Computational Linguistics.

Yuxin Jiang, Linhan Zhang, and Wei Wang. 2022. Global and local hierarchy-aware contrastive framework for implicit discourse relation recognition. *arXiv preprint arXiv:2211.13873*.

Di Jin, Zhijing Jin, Joey Tianyi Zhou, and Peter Szolovits. 2020. Is bert really robust? a strong baseline for natural language attack on text classification and entailment. In *Proceedings of the AAAI conference on artificial intelligence*, volume 34, pages 8018–8025.

Mihir Kale and Abhinav Rastogi. 2020. Text-to-text pre-training for data-to-text tasks. In *Proceedings of the 13th International Conference on Natural Language Generation*, pages 97–102, Dublin, Ireland. Association for Computational Linguistics.

Murathan Kurfalı and Robert Östling. 2019. Zero-shot transfer for implicit discourse relation classification. In *Proceedings of the 20th Annual SIGdial Meeting on Discourse and Dialogue*, pages 226–231, Stockholm, Sweden. Association for Computational Linguistics.

Alex Lascarides and Nicholas Asher. 2007. Segmented discourse representation theory: Dynamic semantics with discourse structure. *Computing meaning*, pages 87–124.

Long Ouyang, Jeffrey Wu, Xu Jiang, Diogo Almeida, Carroll Wainwright, Pamela Mishkin, Chong Zhang, Sandhini Agarwal, Katarina Slama, Alex Ray, et al. 2022. Training language models to follow instructions with human feedback. *Advances in Neural Information Processing Systems*, 35:27730–27744.

Rashmi Prasad, Nikhil Dinesh, Alan Lee, Eleni Miltsakaki, Livio Robaldo, Aravind Joshi, and Bonnie Webber. 2008. The Penn Discourse TreeBank 2.0. In *Proceedings of the Sixth International Conference on Language Resources and Evaluation (LREC'08)*, Marrakech, Morocco. European Language Resources Association (ELRA).

Hugo Touvron, Thibaut Lavril, Gautier Izacard, Xavier Martinet, Marie-Anne Lachaux, Timothée Lacroix, Baptiste Rozière, Naman Goyal, Eric Hambro, Faisal Azhar, et al. 2023. Llama: Open and efficient foundation language models. *arXiv preprint arXiv:2302.13971*.

Frances Yung, Kaveri Anuranjana, Merel Scholman, and Vera Demberg. 2022. Label distributions help implicit discourse relation classification. In *Proceedings of the 3rd Workshop on Computational Approaches to Discourse*, pages 48–53.

Amir Zeldes, Yang Janet Liu, Mikel Iruskieta, Philippe Muller, Chloé Braud, and Sonia Badene. 2021. The disrpt 2021 shared task on elementary discourse unit segmentation, connective detection, and relation classification. In *Proceedings of the 2nd Shared Task on Discourse Relation Parsing and Treebanking (DISRPT 2021)*, pages 1–12.

DisCut and DiscReT: MELODI at DISRPT 2023

[1]Eleni Metheniti and [1,2,3]Chloé Braud and [1,3]Philippe Muller and [1]Laura Rivière
[1]UT3 - IRIT ; [2]CNRS ; [3]ANITI
firstname.lastname@irit.fr

Abstract

This paper presents the results obtained by the MELODI team for the three tasks proposed within the DISRPT 2023 shared task on discourse: segmentation, connective identification, and relation classification. The competition involves corpora in various languages in several underlying frameworks, and proposes two tracks depending on the presence or not of annotations of sentence boundaries and syntactic information. For these three tasks, we rely on a transformer-based architecture, and investigate several optimizations of the models, including hyper-parameter search and layer freezing. For discourse relations, we also explore the use of adapters—a lightweight solution for model fine-tuning—and introduce relation mappings to partially deal with the label set explosion we are facing within the setting of the shared task in a multi-corpus perspective. In the end, we propose one single architecture for segmentation and connectives, based on XLM-RoBERTa large, freezed at lower layers, with new state-of-the-art results for segmentation, and we propose 3 different models for relations, since the task makes it harder to generalize across all corpora.

1 Introduction

Discourse analysis consists in building a discourse structure representing the organization of a document – a monologue or dialogue –, as the discourse tree in Figure 1. First, the document is split into minimal sub-units, called Elementary Discourse Units (EDU): the text in the example, consisting of two sentences, is divided into 5 EDUs (from 2 to 6). The EDUs are then attached together, forming larger discourse units – such as the pair (EDU2, EDU3) – that are recursively linked to form a tree or a graph, depending on the underlying framework. The links between the discourse units are semantic-pragmatic relations, such as CONCESSION, EVIDENCE, SEQUENCE etc. These relations can be triggered by an explicit lexical item, a *connective* such as BECAUSE, WHILE, or WHEN for CONDITION in the example. Relations can also be "implicit", when no such marker is present, such as the CONCESSION between EDU2 and EDU3.

There are mainly three frameworks for discourse: Rhetorical Structure Theory (RST) (Mann and Thompson, 1988) – from which the example in Figure 1 is derived –, Segmented Discourse Theory (SDRT) (Asher and Lascarides, 2003) – where structures are graphs –, and the Penn Discourse Treebank (PDTB) (Prasad et al., 2005), where discourse relations are sparsely annotated without constraints on the overall structure. Alternatively, there have been proposals to transform discourse structure into simpler dependency structures (*dep*), e.g. in RST (Hirao et al., 2013; Hayashi et al., 2016) or SDRT (Muller et al., 2012). Recently, this view has been taken to annotate directly new data in the SciDTB corpus (Yang and Li, 2018), proposing a set of relations and segmentation rules inspired by RST but producing trees of dependency relations between EDUs.

Several corpora have been annotated under each framework for different languages: however, even within the same framework, annotation guidelines and relation sets might be different for each corpus. The DISRPT shared task intends to provide

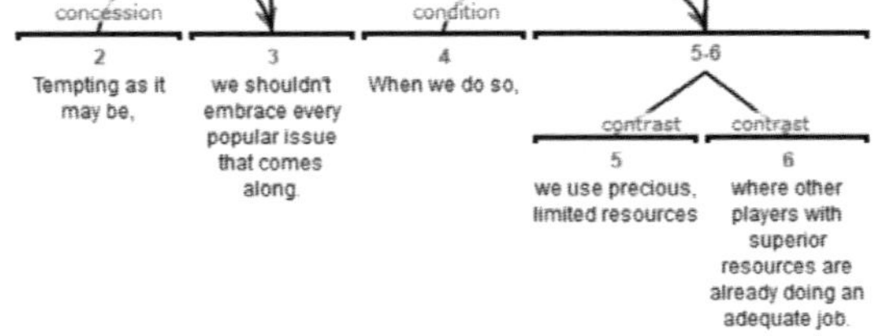

Figure 1: Example of an RST tree (Source: RST website - Common Case Analysis)

Proceedings of the 3rd Shared Task on Discourse Relation Parsing and Treebanking (DISRPT 2023), pages 29–42
July 14, 2023 ©2023 Association for Computational Linguistics

a unified format for researchers to evaluate their systems against varied languages, domains, and frameworks. Three tasks were proposed: (1) discourse segmentation into EDUs, (2) identification of discourse connectives, and (3) classification of discourse relations based on attached units. The first two tasks are encoded with a BIO scheme over tokens, the latter corresponds to a multi-class classification between pairs of textual segments. The benchmark provided within DISRPT allows us to verify the robustness of our approach through 13 languages, 4 frameworks, and varied domains, including multi-party dialogues and speech transcriptions.

In this paper, we address the three tasks through two systems: DisCut[1] for tasks (1) and (2) and DiscReT[2] for task (3). These systems both rely on Transformer architectures and we thoroughly investigate different variations of the pre-trained model and the hyper-parameters values, while also varying the level of frozen layers. This latter parameter allows for lighter models, and also improvements in most cases. For task (3), we also investigate adapters (Houlsby et al., 2019) that provide a lightweight solution for transferring to new tasks. For all tasks, we favor multilingual pretrained models, in order to better generalize and experiment with corpus merging for relations, with the aim of providing a generic model that can be used for any corpus.

In the end, we ranked first on discourse segmentation on the treebanked track ($+0.87$ on the average, compared to the other system) but second for connectives (-0.47), and we are the only system with results on the plain track, with higher performance than the winner of DISRPT 2021. For relations, our system is the only one trying to mix all corpora, thus even if the performance are lower than other proposed approaches, it is possibly better at generalization.

2 Related work

Discourse parsing is the task of building the full trees/graphs. Most work focuses on attachment or discourse relation identification, and on English. Recently, a multilingual RST discourse parser has been proposed (Liu et al., 2021), building on previous work (Braud et al., 2017a; Liu et al., 2020) but proposing to jointly learn attachment and EDU segmentation and adding a cross-lingual strategy, rather than English only. It shows that multilingualism is a key component to improve performance, since data scarcity affects even English, and that good segmentation is crucial, with a loss of up to 8% with predicted EDUs for full parsing.

Discourse segmentation was considered a solved task, with scores as high as 94% (Xuan Bach et al., 2012), but it was later shown that performance drops for languages other than English, – linked to smaller corpora and lesser resources –, and when gold sentences are not given, due to sentence segmenters far from being perfect (Braud et al., 2017b). The first edition of the DISRPT shared task (Zeldes et al., 2019) also revealed the same trend with performance above 95% for some corpora, but also issues with others such as the Spanish SCDT (82.5% at best) or the Russian RRT (86.2%). The best-performing system in 2019 (Muller et al., 2019) was using a single model based on multilingual BERT for every corpus (Devlin et al., 2019), while in the second edition (Zeldes et al., 2021), the best system (Gessler et al., 2021) relied on varied language models, either mono- or multilingual, associated to hand-crafted features: best overall performance was around 91.5% on average, with a loss of about 2% when the sentences are not given.

Connective identification was first seen as a word disambiguation task, where the goal was, starting with a list of candidates, to decide whether each occurrence is used in a discourse reading or not (Pitler et al., 2008). It has been then recast as a sequence labeling one, where we need to decide whether a token starts, is within, or is outside a discourse connective (Stepanov and Riccardi, 2016). As for segmentation, performance drops when existing systems are trained on new domains or languages (Xue et al., 2016; Scholman et al., 2021), but fewer studies investigated this task since implicit relations are more an issue for discourse parsing. The first two editions of DISRPT demonstrated rather high performance: between $92-94$ for the English and Turkish corpora, and 87 for the Chinese one, with only a small drop when sentences are not given.

Discourse relations are the main object of study within the domain, with a specific focus on implicit ones since the connective is considered a very strong clue for guessing the relation (Pitler et al., 2008). However, again, performance drops, even for explicit relations when data are scarce (Jo-

[1] Code at `https://github.com/phimit/jiant/`

[2] Code at `https://gitlab.irit.fr/melodi/andiamo/discret_ST3`

hannsen and Søgaard, 2013). Moreover, a real-life scenario has to deal with both implicit and explicit relations, it is thus interesting to see results combining all types of relations, and for several languages. Only two systems were presented in 2021, and the winning model was based on Transformers, with a specific pretrained model depending on the target language and additional hand-crafted features: best overall performance is still low, with 61.8%.

3 Data

The 2023 DISRPT shared task, including suprise datasets, provides 26 corpora for 13 languages and 4 theoretical frameworks: 9 correspond to the PDTB framework (thus connective and relations), the others are either RST (12), dependency (3) or SDRT (2) (thus segmentation and relations). Among these, 10 new corpora are introduced in the 2023 edition: 6 are released as surprise datasets, with one new language (Thaï), and out-of-domain (OOD) data for English (COVID-DTB and TED), Portuguese (CRPC and TED) and Turkish (TED).

All statistics are given in Table 1. The largest corpora are the English PDTB (1, 992 training documents), dep SciDTB (492 documents), and RST DT (309 training documents), and, for SDRT, the French Annodis (64 documents). In total, 8 corpora have less than 100 documents and are thus considered very small. The OOD corpora have no training set: the English COVDTB is rather large, with 150 in the dev set, but the other ones, based on TED talks for English, Portuguese, and Turkish are very small, their dev sets contain only 2 documents, around 100 connectives, and 200 relations to predict. For relations, label sets contain between 9 and 32 different relations, and we note that almost no corpus has the same set as another one.

We have 6 corpora for English (Prasad et al., 2019; Zeldes, 2017; Carlson et al., 2001; Asher et al., 2016; Yang and Li, 2018; Nishida and Matsumoto, 2022), 4 for Chinese (Zhou et al., 2014; Cao et al., 2018; Cheng and Li, 2019; Yi et al., 2021), 2 for Spanish (da Cunha et al., 2011; Cao et al., 2018), 2 for Portuguese (Cardoso et al., 2011; Mendes and Lejeune, 2022), 1 for German (Stede and Neumann, 2014), 1 for Basque (Iruskieta et al., 2013), 1 for Farsi (Shahmohammadi et al., 2021), 1 for French (Afantenos et al., 2012), 1 for Dutch (Redeker et al., 2012), 1 for Russian (Toldova et al., 2017), 1 for Turkish (Zeyrek and Webber, 2008; Zeyrek and Kurfalı, 2017), 1 for Italian (Tonelli et al., 2010; Riccardi et al., 2016) and 1 for Thai. In addition, OOD datasets come from the multilingual TED Discourse Bank with data for English, Portuguese and Turkish (Zeyrek et al., 2018, 2020).

4 DisCut: segmentation and connectives

4.1 DisCut: Model architecture

Identifying EDU boundaries and connectives (Tasks 1 and 2) corresponds to different corpora: PDTB-based datasets have connectives annotated, but not segmentation, while the others have no connectives. However, they can be both modeled as sequence labeling tasks (only "Beginning" labels for segmentation, "Beginning" and also "Inside" for connectives, to take into account multi-words markers). Our systems for these tasks are thus based on the same architecture with transformers pretrained models, fine-tuned on the task at hand.

The model is based on a pretrained language model (LM), with an additional linear layer for token classification. The LM is multilingual, allowing it to be used for all corpora. Contrary to systems proposed in 2019 and 2021 based on a similar architecture, we removed the CNN at the character level, and the LSTM outer layer, as additional experiments demonstrated no improvements.

The LM is based on a Transformer architecture with several layers within the encoder. It has been shown that, broadly speaking, lower layers mostly encode morpho-syntactic information, while upper contain more semantic ones (Rogers et al., 2020; Kovaleva et al., 2019; Bender and Koller, 2020). We thus experiment with freezing some lower layers while continuing the fine-tuning on higher levels, in order to have lighter models. "Freezing a layer" is the process of disallowing the update of weights for the target layer during the fine-tuning process, meaning that the layer preserves its learned information from pretraining.

Models are fed with sentences, the documents being too long for the LMs. We detail below our setting when sentences are not given ('Plain' track).

4.2 Settings

We chose to focus on multilingual LMs and experimented with mBERT (Devlin et al., 2019) and XLM-RoBERTa (Conneau et al., 2020). We present results using XLM-RoBERTa, as preliminary experiments demonstrated improvements over mBERT. We experimented with both *base* and *large* versions, and tested the freezing of lower

Corpus	Train				Dev				Test			
	#Doc	#Tok	#EDU/Conn	#Rel	#Doc	#Tok	#EDU/Conn	#Rel	#Doc	#Tok	#EDU/Conn	#Rel
						RST						
eng.rst.rstdt	309	166854	17646	17/16002	38	17309	1797	17/1621	38	21666	2346	17/2155
rus.rst.rrt	272	390375	34682	22/28868	30	40779	3352	19/2855	30	41851	3508	20/2843
spa.rst.rststb	203	43055	2472	28/2240	32	7551	419	23/383	32	8111	460	25/426
eng.rst.gum	165	160700	20722	14/19496	24	21409	2790	14/2617	24	21770	2740	14/2575
deu.rst.pcc	142	26831	2449	26/2164	17	3152	275	24/241	17	3239	294	24/260
fas.rst.prstc	120	52309	4607	17/4100	15	7016	576	15/499	15	7369	670	16/592
eus.rst.ert	116	30690	2785	29/2533	24	7219	677	26/614	24	7871	740	26/678
por.rst.cstn	114	48469	4601	32/4148	14	6509	630	22/573	12	3815	306	21/272
nld.rst.nldt	56	17562	1662	32/1608	12	3783	343	27/331	12	3553	338	28/325
zho.rst.gcdt	40	47639	7470	31/6454	5	7619	1144	30/1006	5	7647	1092	30/953
spa.rst.sctb	32	10253	473	24/439	9	2448	103	17/94	9	3814	168	19/159
zho.rst.sctb	32	9655	473	26/439	9	2264	103	19/94	9	3577	168	20/159
						SDRT						
fra.sdrt.annodis	64	22515	2255	18/2185	11	5013	556	18/528	11	5171	618	18/625
eng.sdrt.stac	33	41060	9887	16/9580	6	4747	1154	16/1145	6	6547	1547	16/1510
						DEP						
eng.dep.scidtb	492	62461	6740	24/6060	154	20288	2130	24/1933	152	19744	2116	24/1911
∗eng.dep.covdtb	-	-	-	-	150	29369	2754	12/2399	150	31480	2951	12/2586
zho.dep.scidtb	69	11288	898	23/802	20	3852	309	18/281	20	3621	235	17/215
						PDTB						
eng.pdtb.pdtb	1992	1061229	23850	23/43920	79	39768	953	20/1674	91	55660	1245	23/2257
por.pdtb.crpc	243	147594	3994	22/8797	28	20102	621	20/1285	31	19153	544	19/1248
tur.pdtb.tdb	159	391304	7063	23/2451	19	49097	831	22/312	19	46988	854	22/422
∗tha.pdtb.tdtb	139	199135	8277	20/8278	19	27326	1243	18/1243	22	30062	1344	18/1344
zho.pdtb.cdtb	125	52061	1034	9/3657	21	11178	314	9/855	18	10075	312	9/758
ita.pdtb.luna	42	16776	671	15/956	6	3081	139	14/210	12	6257	261	14/381
∗eng.pdtb.tedm	-	-	-	-	2	2574	110	20/178	4	5474	231	18/351
∗por.pdtb.tedm	-	-	-	-	2	2785	102	20/190	4	5405	203	18/364
∗tur.pdtb.tedm	-	-	-	-	2	2113	135	21/213	4	4030	247	22/364

Table 1: Statistics on the datasets: **bold** indicates a new corpus compared to DISRPT 2021, ∗ indicates a surprise corpus, '-' is for OOD corpora, without training sets. #EDU/CONN is the number of EDUs for RST, SDRT, and DEP corpora, the number of connectives for PDTB corpora; #REL corresponds to the size of label sets / total number of pairs annotated.

layers, aiming at possibly improved performance, with a lighter training.

With XLM-RoBERTa base, we tested no freezing, or freezing of either the first 3 or 8 layers (out of 12); for the large version, we increased to 6 and 12 layers (out of 24). We tested several values for the learning rate $\in [10^{-5}, 2\cdot10^{-5}, 10^{-4}]$ and chose 10^{-5}. We tested different batch sizes $\in [1, 4, 8, 16]$ – only the value 1 fitted our GPU for the large version –, with a gradient accumulation of 4 and a maximum of 30 epochs with patience of 10 over the performance on the development set. The input size is limited to 180. Our implementation relies on and extends the Jiant library[3] (Phang et al., 2020).

After evaluation on the dev set, we found that most models perform better with RoBERTa-large and with freezing the first 6 layers. Small improvements could be observed for some corpora with either the base version or other freezing values, but the increase was limited to less than 1.2%, and in general less than .5%, and we thus decided to favor one single model in order to make it easier to use, and better at generalizing to new data.

Dealing with raw data: The DISRPT shared task proposes two tracks for tasks 1 and 2: you can either use data segmented into sentences and syntactically parsed (*Treebanked*) – either gold or obtained with Stanza –, or raw tokenized documents (*Plain*). As the LMs have limitations on the size of their input, we can not give directly the documents as input: we thus decided to split the raw documents into sentences.

However, having observed issues with Stanza segmentation, we tried alternatives: Ersatz (Wicks and Post, 2021) and Trankit (Nguyen et al., 2021), and chose the latter based on better performance. Note that, with the evaluation being based on tokens, we had to realign tokens when the tool was modifying the tokenization. We were unable to obtain a correct sentence segmentation for the Italian ita.pdtb.luna, composed of speech transcripts, and

[3]`https://jiant.info/`

thus cut every 120 tokens for this corpus.

Dealing with surprise and OOD data: Dealing with the surprise Thai (tha.pdtb.tdtb) and English (eng.dep.covdtb) datasets were straightforward: since our model configuration is the same across all corpora, we retrain new models using the training data made available. This year, the organizers also include out-of-domain (OOD) data as surprise datasets, for which data are only available for evaluation (dev and test sets only). The corpora have, however, corresponding datasets within the same framework and language: we use our model trained on these available data to make predictions on the OOD ones (e.g. training on eng.pdtb.pdtb to test on eng.pdtb.tedm).

4.3 Experiments and results

We present our results in Table 2 for segmentation and connective identification. Current comparison with 2021, considering only the corpora available in 2021, demonstrate general improvements for all tasks except connective for the Plain track were results are on par: for segmentation, the average on test sets for Treebanked is 91.77% (vs 91.48 for DiscoDisco 2021) and for Plain 91.22% (vs 89.79); for connective: 91.81% (vs 91.22) for Treebanked and 91.05% (vs 91.49) for Plain. Note that our approach uses a similar architecture with much simpler inputs (only tokens), and different optimizations. When comparing the reproduced results with the ones we produced, we observed a large variance between the scores, especially for small corpora, with for example a difference of about 2 to 5 points for the TEDm corpora, and about 2 to 3 points also for other small datasets such as the spa.rst.sctb, the zho.rst.sctb, demonstrating the importance for future work to make multiple runs and indicate variance. Interested readers can find our own results on the test sets in Appendix A.

As shown in Table 2, compared to 2021, we observe a large drop in mean performance of about 10% for connective detection, for which many new corpora were added, including several OOD datasets making the task more challenging.

For segmentation, the results for the two settings, Treebanked and Plain are in general very similar, except for the Chinese zho.rst.sctb and English eng.sdrt.stac for which the Treebanked setting is clearly better (+3 to 5%). On the other hand, we have an important improvement for the French corpus fra.sdrt.annodis (almost +3%) using our new

Corpus	Treebanked			Plain		
	F1 dev	F1 test	DD21	F1 dev	F1 test	DD21
			Segmentation			
deu.rst.pcc	96.79	**96.01**	95.58	96.60	**94.24**	93.94
eng.rst.gum	95.54	**95.50**	94.15	95.78	**94.46**	92.61
eng.rst.rstdt	97.33	**97.62**	96.64	97.60	**97.74**	96.35
eus.rst.ert	91.69	89.93	**90.46**	91.83	**91.09**	90.47
fas.rst.prstc	93.79	**93.40**	92.94	94.05	**93.36**	92.86
nld.rst.nldt	97.51	**96.54**	95.97	97.09	**97.19**	94.69
por.rst.cstn	94.06	93.98	**94.35**	93.50	**94.36**	94.11
rus.rst.rrt	86.80	85.58	**86.21**	84.75	85.41	**85.74**
spa.rst.rststb	96.19	**93.53**	92.22	96.32	**93.70**	91.76
spa.rst.sctb	86.88	**85.63**	82.48	85.44	**84.21**	80.86
zho.rst.gcdt	92.69	92.55	-	92.20	91.74	-
zho.rst.sctb	79.05	81.84	**83.34**	77.53	**78.55**	76.21
eng.sdrt.stac	94.77	**95.22**	94.91	91.57	90.67	**91.91**
fra.sdrt.annodis	90.27	88.21	**90.02**	90.17	**90.89**	85.78
∗**eng.dep.covdtb**	91.32	92.13	-	91.65	92.13	-
eng.dep.scidtb	96.18	95.07	-	95.63	94.49	-
zho.dep.scidtb	93.33	89.07	-	93.01	90.04	-
Mean	92.60	91.87	-	92.04	91.43	-
Mean corpora 2021	-	**91.77**	91.48	-	**91.22**	89.79
			Connective identification			
eng.pdtb.pdtb	94.41	**93.66**	92.02	93.94	91.64	**92.56**
∗**eng.pdtb.tedm**	75.86	78.36	-	80.00	75.83	-
ita.pdtb.luna	79.72	65.85	-	74.19	71.60	-
por.pdtb.crpc	85.16	80.66	-	84.65	79.49	-
∗**por.pdtb.tedm**	73.08	80.29	-	71.22	79.45	-
∗**tha.pdtb.tdtb**	87.43	85.66	-	74.32	69.92	-
tur.pdtb.tdb	89.73	92.77	**94.11**	89.69	91.12	**93.56**
∗**tur.pdtb.tedm**	65.42	64.10	-	64.15	64.78	-
zho.pdtb.cdtb	87.66	**89.00**	87.52	87.77	**90.38**	88.35
Mean	82.05	81.15	-	79.99	79.36	-
Mean corpora 2021	-	**91.81**	91.22	-	91.05	**91.49**

Table 2: DisCut: Results (F1) on the dev and test sets for segmentation and discourse connective identification. Models with XLM-RoBERTa-large, freezing layers 0-5. Test scores come from the reproduction done by the organizers. 'DD21' stands for DiscoDisco 2021, the system ranked first in DISRPT 2021. 'Mean corpora 2021' is the mean F1 without considering the corpora added in DISRPT 2023.

segmented files (Plain): these results are in line with the bad performance observed for Stanza. For the Russian corpus, we found that the segmentation of some parts of the documents was strange: bibliography entries were merged into very large EDUs that were split by all sentence segmenters, thus modifying the tool did not bring any improvement.

For connective detection, results are rather high for large corpora already present in the previous campaigns, even if the Chinese corpus is still challenging. As expected, the Italian Luna is associated with low performance, because it is composed of speech transcriptions of dialogues. Note that the performance for the new Thai corpus is on par, but they drop on the out-of-domain TEDm corpora for which we used the model trained on a corpus with the same language and framework, but that corresponds to a domain shift. Interestingly, the use of Trankit for sentence segmentation (Plain track) leads to large improvements for Luna (almost +6%) and also allows a small increase for the Chinese zho.pdtb.cdtb (+1.4), with, on the other hand, a loss of about 2% for the English PDTB, and an impressive drop of about 16% for Thai for which the model of sentence segmentation is probably faulty. Overall, the Plain setting would lead to average results on par with the treebanked ones for connective identification, without the Thai dataset (80.54 on average for Plain against 80.59 for Treebanked, without Thai). These results indicate that the good performance of the sentence segmenter is a key component of a well performing discourse segmenter or connective identifier.

5 DiscReT: Discourse Relation Tagging

5.1 Introduction

For the third proposed task, Discourse Relation Classification across Formalisms, we submit a multilingual approach to discourse relation tagging that spans across frameworks, powered by transformer-based architectures. Our goal is to test the capacities and weaknesses of these models, given the large variety of languages and relation labels, without sacrificing the multilingual setting or the unique information captured in coarse-/fine-grained labels. Our results vary vastly between languages and frameworks but present interesting pointers for future work and model improvements.

5.2 Dataset

In order to stay faithful to the multilingual nature of the task, we decided to use all the datasets in parallel for training. Extensive earlier experiments with translations of the datasets to English, training with groups of corpora per language family, or training per annotation framework were not as successful or did not significantly outperform the accumulative approach.

We aimed to reduce label space and maximize label coverage, i.e. not having a label that only exists in one corpus if it can be rewritten as a more general one. First, we lower-cased all labels in all datasets (but preserved our modifications, in order to reverse them for the final results in accordance with the Shared Task data). Second, we manually merged labels that were either spelling variants or simplified versions of existing labels. For example, the label "qap" means "question-answer pair", which already exists as the label "question_answer_pair". Meanwhile, the label "conjunction" is a simplified version of the label "expansion.conjunction" found in RST corpora in both forms, therefore by changing the label to its more verbose form, we are preserving its information and making the labels more uniform. However, we decided against the large-scale conversion of labels based on their meaning, e.g. merging the "conjunction" and "joint" labels.These conversions reduced the number of unique labels from 163 to 135; while the number was not significantly reduced, we wanted to make the results more interpretable without sacrificing important information. We present the implemented conversions in Table 3.

Original Label	**Conversion**
alternation	expansion.alternative
alternative	expansion.alternative
bg-general	background
causation	cause
cause-result	cause-effect
conditional	condition
conjunction	expansion.conjunction
correction	expansion.correction
disjunction	expansion.disjunction
evidence	explanation-evidence
exp-evidence	explanation-evidence
expansion.genexpansion	expansion
expansion.level	expansion.level-of-detail
findings	result
goal	purpose-goal
joint-disjunction	expansion.disjunction
justify	explanation-justify
list	joint-list
motivation	explanation-motivation
otherwise	adversative
qap	question_answer_pair
qap.hypophora	hypophora
repetition	restatement-repetition
restatement	expansion.restatement
sequence	joint-sequence
temporal.synchrony	temporal.synchronous
textual-organization	organization
unconditional	expansion.disjunction
unless	contrast

Table 3: List of label conversions that we implemented (apart from lower-casing). Underlined labels were found exclusively in the surprise datasets.

We make use of the directional information of the relations, available in the datasets in the column "dir". We do not change the input in sentences with the direction "1>2", but we switch the input position of sentences with the direction "1<2" to "2>1". An example can be found in Table 4. Even though the models we use in this task are bidirectional, we observed an increase in performance when the direction of relations was unified.

We do not further process the text input, as the

Corpus:	spa.rst.rststb
unit1_txt	La diferenciación como un modelo para el análisis de las relaciones de pareja
unit2_txt	El presente artículo hace una revisión sobre este concepto
dir	1>2
label	preparation
input	[CLS] La diferenciación como un modelo para el análisis de las relaciones de pareja [SEP] El presente artículo hace una revisión sobre este concepto

Corpus:	deu.rst.pcc
unit1_txt	Und die Zeit drängt .
unit2_txt	Der große Einbruch der Schülerzahlen an den weiterführenden Schulen beginnt bereits im Herbst 2003 .
dir	1<2
label	reason
input	[CLS] Der große Einbruch der Schülerzahlen an den weiterführenden Schulen beginnt bereits im Herbst 2003 . [SEP] Und die Zeit drängt .

Table 4: Examples of inputs with different directions. In the first example, the direction of the relation is 1>2, therefore the model input is in the same order as in the data. In the second example, the direction is 1<2, so the model input has the two sentences in reversed order.

necessary conversions (e.g. tokenization, lowercasing) are specified by each model. However, at the tokenization stage, we ensured that the input length complied with the restrictions of maximum input length that transformer-based models impose; each sentence is truncated to half of the maximum input length, if necessary.

5.3 DiscReT: Model architectures

We opted for transformer-based architectures for our experiments and tested several of them (mBERT, xml-RoBERTa, DistilBERT) in order to decide on which one to focus our research effort on. After preliminary tests, the multilingual BERT base cased model (mBERT) (Devlin et al., 2019) was the most successful overall and included all the languages of the Shared Task in its pretrained version available from Huggingface.[4]

As a "baseline" for our experiments, we trained an mBERT classifier built with PyTorch (Paszke et al., 2019), without frozen layers, and trained for a maximum of 5 epochs.

In order to inject additional information in the finetuning process of the classifier, without further changing the input data, we used *adapters* alongside our mBERT classifier. Adapters (Houlsby et al., 2019) are an alternative lightweight method to finetuning with equivalent good results on most NLP tasks. An adapter is a transformer architecture with layer-specific pretrained parameters Θ_l which are frozen and a small set of new parameters Φ_l (where l is the transformer layer). During finetuning, only the adapters' Φ_l parameters are updated from the loss function L on dataset D (see Equation 1). This enables efficient parameter sharing between tasks, languages, etc.

$$\Phi_l^* \leftarrow \arg\min_{\Phi_l} L(D; \{\Theta_l, \Phi_l\}) \quad (1)$$

We are using the tool AdapterHub (Pfeiffer et al., 2020) which allows for easier finetuning and integration of adapters to transformer-based models. After several experiments, we observed that the finetuning process of an adapter is quite different than that of a model; the adapter set of parameters learns most effectively with more finetuning epochs than a normal model and the training process per epoch is longer. Additionally, we experimented with freezing the parameters of certain layers for the models and the adapters, in order to determine the best model.

We trained multiple mBERT adapters, out of which the most successful were:

1. mBERT adapter trained on the entire dataset for 15 epochs and with frozen layer 1 (A1)
2. mBERT adapter trained on the entire dataset for 15 epochs and with frozen layers 1-3 (A1-3)

5.4 Results

5.4.1 Shared Task results

While evaluating our models, we observed that the best accuracy in each development set was not always achieved by one model. Our final submission is composed of three models:

1. the "baseline" finetuned mBERT model without adapter with multiple epochs (B)
2. the finetuned mBERT model for 3 epochs with an mBERT adapter trained for 15 epochs and layer 1 frozen (A1)
3. the finetuned mBERT-cased model for 4 epochs with an mBERT adapter trained for 15 epochs and layers 1-3 frozen (A1-3)

The results on the test set, as recreated and reported by the organizers of the Shared Task, are found in Table 5. Our poor performance is, to some

[4]https://huggingface.co/bert-base-multilingual-cased

extent, due to the problems we faced to convert the lower-cased and converted labels back to their upper-cased format, which was required for the Shared Task evaluation. This dramatically lowered the test results reproduced and published for the Shared Task. For clarity, we are reporting the Shared Task results from the organizers, but also include the results on the dev and test sets that were produced before converting the labels to their original in Tables 6 and 7 respectively. These results were calculated with scikit-learn (Pedregosa et al., 2011) and the process of calculating them is transparent in our code.

Our goal was to create a truly multilingual approach for discourse relation parsing. We did not aim to establish a new state-of-the-art, but to observe whether multilingual word embeddings can work in synergy (to learn common labels) and specialize at the same time (to learn corpus-unique labels). We also deliberately focused and submitted a combination of three models, instead of proposing the best model for each dataset, thus sacrificing performance for reproducibility. During our experiments, there were other combinations of adapters and models with frozen layers that yielded slightly better results on specific corpora, however, the training times for multiple models would be problematic for a Shared Task entry.

Given that our results are not much worse than approaches with a combination of monolingual models and independent training, it is possible to derive benefits from joint training and evaluating multiple languages. Our multilingual models showed strengths (e.g. in the spa.rst.rstsb dataset) and weaknesses (e.g. in English, Turkish and Chinese datasets) that cannot be pinpointed directly to a specific framework, the size of the corpus, or the size of the specific language data, and will need to be further explored. Our submission was marred by implementation issues, but we are hopeful that in future work we will tackle these issues and implement improvements on our multilingual approach.

Corpus	DiscReT	DiscoDisco	Difference
deu.rst.pcc	26.92	39.23	-12.31
eng.rst.gum	55.34	66.76	-11.42
eng.rst.rstdt	49.98	67.1	-17.12
eus.rst.ert	51.77	60.62	-8.85
fas.rst.prstc	50.34	52.53	-2.19
nld.rst.nldt	43.69	55.21	-11.52
por.rst.cstn	62.87	64.34	-1.47
rus.rst.rrt	61.52	66.44	-4.92
spa.rst.rststb	58.22	54.23	**3.99**
spa.rst.sctb	33.33	66.04	-32.71
zho.rst.gcdt	55.72	-	-
zho.rst.sctb	49.06	64.15	-15.09
eng.sdrt.stac	56.89	65.03	-8.14
fra.sdrt.annodis	44.96	46.4	-1.44
∗**eng.dep.covdtb**	41.3	-	-
eng.dep.scidtb	67.56	-	-
zho.dep.scidtb	67.44	-	-
eng.pdtb.pdtb	69.25	74.44	-5.19
∗**eng.pdtb.tedm**	19.94	-	-
ita.pdtb.luna	58.42	-	-
∗**por.pdtb.crpc**	72.76	-	-
∗**por.pdtb.tedm**	54.95	-	-
∗**tha.pdtb.tdtb**	95.24	-	-
tur.pdtb.tdb	49.05	60.09	-11.04
∗**tur.pdtb.tedm**	49.73	-	-
zho.pdtb.cdtb	69.13	86.49	-17.36
MEAN (all)	54.44	-	
MEAN (2021)	52.02	61.82	-9.8

Table 5: The results that organizers provided for discourse relation classification (Task 3), evaluating the test sets and reporting accuracy in %. 'DiscoDisco' was the best-performing model of DISRPT 2021 (Gessler et al., 2021) and 'Diff.' is the comparison with our models. MEAN (all) provides the mean for the currently available datasets, while MEAN (2021) averages only DISRPT 2021's corpora.

6 Conclusion

In this paper, we presented our submissions for the three tasks of the DISRPT Shared Task. Our main goals were to rely on only a few architectures variants for generality, and experiment with parameter efficient methods. For Tasks 1-2, we employed multi-task, multi-corpora approaches; however, at this stage of our research our results are not optimal. In future work, we aim to further explore this strategy, as it seems promising for lower-resource languages. Additionally, we are interested in approaches beyond the scope of this campaign, such as domain transfer. Furthermore, it was possible to perform segmentation and connective detection on datasets without training data, as shown by the surprise TEDm test sets. It would be interesting to examine whether the DISRPT framework could be transferred to new languages, for which there are no training data for segmentation or connective detection, such as the rest of the TEDm corpus. As for Task 3, our focus was on a unified, purely multilingual approach with parameter optimization, as well as dataset preprocessing for unification. Even though we faced problems on the Shared Task submission results, our approach showed promising results compared to language-specific models.

Corpus	B (1)	B (2)	B (3)	B (4)	B (5)	B (6)	A1-3 (4)	A1 (3)
deu.rst.pcc	25.31	29.46	26.97	**31.54**	31.54	29.88	29.05	30.71
eng.rst.gum	48.03	51.66	52.46	53.31	53.76	53.69	55.79	**56.67**
eng.rst.rstdt	46.33	49.85	44.97	47.25	48.49	47.62	**51.02**	50.28
eus.rst.ert	41.53	43.65	43.16	44.95	42.18	44.46	45.44	**47.07**
fas.rst.prstc	**53.31**	50.1	52.1	51.3	49.5	51.9	52.91	52.71
nld.rst.nldt	43.5	40.79	**46.53**	41.09	46.53	42.9	45.92	45.32
por.rst.cstn	54.8	59.51	55.15	60.38	60.56	58.12	**62.48**	61.43
rus.rst.rrt	57.41	58.84	60.04	60.04	58.77	59.61	**61.16**	60.91
spa.rst.rststb	51.44	54.31	55.61	**62.4**	60.05	61.62	60.31	59.01
spa.rst.sctb	47.87	62.77	56.38	58.51	62.77	**67.02**	59.57	64.89
zho.rst.gcdt	53.98	55.57	56.86	57.55	57.75	58.05	58.85	**59.34**
zho.rst.sctb	40.43	**50**	46.81	46.81	42.55	**50**	47.87	46.81
eng.sdrt.stac	45.5	55.02	53.8	55.28	55.55	54.15	**57.82**	56.59
fra.sdrt.annodis	30.3	44.32	47.16	46.4	**49.81**	47.92	48.3	47.54
∗eng.dep.covdtb	40.39	42.81	35.22	36.64	36.18	42.93	**43.56**	43.1
eng.dep.scidtb	59.39	59.34	66.48	66.06	70.2	66.17	70.56	**71.03**
zho.dep.scidtb	47.33	61.57	62.99	59.79	60.85	62.63	**66.19**	65.48
eng.pdtb.pdtb	67.32	67.44	71.39	70.85	70.43	69.41	**72.4**	71.09
∗eng.pdtb.tedm	10.67	14.04	19.1	15.73	15.17	14.04	**20.79**	19.1
ita.pdtb.luna	45.93	53.59	51.67	50.72	54.07	54.07	54.55	**56.46**
∗por.pdtb.crpc	65.76	66.69	67.39	67.16	67.16	65.29	**68.25**	67.94
∗por.pdtb.tedm	50	45.79	47.37	49.47	48.95	46.32	**54.21**	51.05
∗tha.pdtb.tdtb	92.68	93.56	93.08	93.97	93.64	92.76	93.72	**93.97**
tur.pdtb.tdb	42.95	39.1	**42.95**	40.06	39.42	41.67	41.03	39.1
∗tur.pdtb.tedm	42.72	42.72	44.13	42.25	41.31	**46.48**	43.66	43.66
zho.pdtb.cdtb	73.8	75.09	**76.37**	74.62	73.8	74.15	75.44	73.92
MEAN	49.18	52.6	52.93	53.24	53.5	53.96	**55.42**	55.2

Table 6: Results on the dev set for discourse relation classification, before converting labels to their original form. In parenthesis is the number of epochs for which the model was trained.

Corpus	B (1)	B (2)	B (3)	B (4)	B (5)	B (6)	A1-3 (4)	A1 (3)	DiscoDisco	Diff.
deu.rst.pcc	25.77	30.77	26.54	32.31	32.31	33.08	**33.85**	33.08	39.23	-5.38
eng.rst.gum	50.49	54.72	55.96	57.09	57.36	55.69	**58.56**	58.41	66.76	-8.2
eng.rst.rstdt	46.91	**50.16**	46.73	47.94	48.54	48.77	49.84	49.88	67.1	-16.94
eus.rst.ert	40.56	43.66	44.99	47.94	46.17	48.97	50.44	**51.33**	60.62	-9.29
fas.rst.prstc	47.47	47.13	48.31	**50.84**	47.47	49.16	50.51	49.66	52.53	-1.69
nld.rst.nldt	43.38	42.46	43.38	42.46	43.38	40.31	46.15	**47.38**	55.21	-7.83
por.rst.cstn	64.34	65.44	65.07	64.34	63.97	64.71	**65.44**	65.07	64.34	**1.1**
rus.rst.rrt	59.44	60.11	60.75	60.96	60.11	59.41	**62.29**	61.98	66.44	-4.15
spa.rst.rststb	48.83	51.17	53.76	57.04	54.69	53.76	57.75	**59.15**	54.23	**4.92**
spa.rst.sctb	58.49	64.15	64.78	**69.81**	64.15	63.52	65.41	61.64	66.04	**3.77**
zho.rst.gcdt	47.32	49.32	49.32	52.78	53.2	52.47	53.73	**54.67**	-	-
zho.rst.sctb	45.28	53.46	55.35	**57.86**	44.03	48.43	47.8	50.31	64.15	-6.29
eng.sdrt.stac	40.99	50.46	50.73	52.52	52.32	51.19	**55.76**	55.17	65.03	-9.27
fra.sdrt.annodis	31.68	42.56	45.92	44	44.8	45.12	**46.88**	45.12	46.4	**0.48**
∗eng.dep.covdtb	38.09	**41.38**	33.37	35.11	35.77	39.44	41.14	40.87	-	-
eng.dep.scidtb	59.45	61.38	67.29	67.09	69.65	68.18	69.81	**70.38**	-	-
zho.dep.scidtb	53.02	61.86	64.19	56.28	60.93	60.93	**64.65**	64.19	-	-
eng.pdtb.pdtb	64.91	64.2	68.41	68.01	65.62	64.82	**68.85**	68.63	74.44	-5.59
∗eng.pdtb.tedm	10.83	12.25	18.23	15.67	12.54	15.67	**20.8**	19.94	-	-
ita.pdtb.luna	45.53	52.11	52.11	52.37	56.32	53.68	57.63	**57.63**	-	-
∗por.pdtb.crpc	69.15	67.71	70.59	71.07	70.67	68.51	71.07	**72.04**	-	-
∗por.pdtb.tedm	58.24	54.12	58.52	56.04	55.49	56.04	56.32	**58.52**	-	-
∗tha.pdtb.tdtb	94.12	95.16	95.24	**95.39**	95.16	94.79	94.94	95.31	-	-
tur.pdtb.tdb	**51.9**	48.1	48.82	48.58	46.92	50.95	51.42	50.71	60.09	-8.19
∗tur.pdtb.tedm	45.33	45.05	44.51	45.33	44.23	46.7	49.18	**50.55**	-	-
zho.pdtb.cdtb	68.34	71.24	**73.61**	67.41	66.75	65.17	68.6	66.89	86.49	-12.88
MEAN (2021)	49.3	52.49	53.32	54.32	52.41	52.69	**54.97**	54.65	61.82	-7.17
MEAN (all)	50.38	53.08	54.1	54.47	53.56	53.83	**56.11**	56.1	-	-

Table 7: Results on the test set for discourse relation classification, before converting labels to their original form. In parenthesis is the number of epochs for which the model was trained. 'DiscoDisco' was the best-performing model of DISRPT 2021 (Gessler et al., 2021) and 'Diff.' is the comparison with our models. MEAN (all) provides the mean for the currently available datasets, while MEAN (2021) averages only DISRPT 2021's corpora.

Acknowledgements

This work is supported by the AnDiaMO project (ANR-21-CE23-0020). This work was partially supported by the ANR (ANR-19-PI3A-0004) through the AI Interdisciplinary Institute, ANITI, as a part of France's "Investing for the Future — PIA3" program. This work is also partially supported by the SLANT project (ANR-19-CE23-0022). Chloé Braud and Philippe Muller are part of the programme DesCartes and are also supported by the National Research Foundation, Prime Minister's Office, Singapore under its Campus for Research Excellence and Technological Enterprise (CREATE) programme. The work was also supported by the ANR grant SUMM-RE (ANR-20-CE23-0017).

References

Stergos Afantenos, Nicholas Asher, Farah Benamara, Anaïs Cadilhac, Cédric Degremont, Pascal Denis, Markus Guhe, Simon Keizer, Alex Lascarides, Oliver Lemon, Philippe Muller, Soumya Paul, Verena Rieser, and Laure Vieu. 2012. Developing a corpus of strategic conversation in the settlers of catan. In *Proceedings of the workshop on Games and NLP (GAMNLP)*.

Nicholas Asher, Julie Hunter, Mathieu Morey, Benamara Farah, and Stergos Afantenos. 2016. Discourse structure and dialogue acts in multiparty dialogue: the STAC corpus. In *Proceedings of the Tenth International Conference on Language Resources and Evaluation (LREC'16)*, pages 2721–2727, Portorož, Slovenia. European Language Resources Association (ELRA).

Nicholas Asher and Alex Lascarides. 2003. *Logics of Conversation*. Cambridge University Press.

Emily M. Bender and Alexander Koller. 2020. Climbing towards NLU: On meaning, form, and understanding in the age of data. In *Proceedings of the 58th Annual Meeting of the Association for Computational Linguistics*, pages 5185–5198, Online. Association for Computational Linguistics.

Chloé Braud, Maximin Coavoux, and Anders Søgaard. 2017a. Cross-lingual RST discourse parsing. In *Proceedings of the 15th Conference of the European Chapter of the Association for Computational Linguistics: Volume 1, Long Papers*, pages 292–304, Valencia, Spain. Association for Computational Linguistics.

Chloé Braud, Ophélie Lacroix, and Anders Søgaard. 2017b. Cross-lingual and cross-domain discourse segmentation of entire documents. In *Proceedings of the 55th Annual Meeting of the Association for Computational Linguistics (Volume 2: Short Papers)*, pages 237–243, Vancouver, Canada. Association for Computational Linguistics.

Shuyuan Cao, Iria da Cunha, and Mikel Iruskieta. 2018. The RST Spanish-Chinese treebank. In *Proceedings of the Joint Workshop on Linguistic Annotation, Multiword Expressions and Constructions (LAW-MWE-CxG-2018)*, pages 156–166, Santa Fe, New Mexico, USA. Association for Computational Linguistics.

Paula Christina Figueira Cardoso, Erick Galani Maziero, Maria Lucía del Rosario Castro Jorge, M. Eloize, R. Kibar Aji Seno, Ariani Di Felippo, Lucia Helena Machado Rino, Maria das Graças Volpe Nunes, and Thiago Alexandre Salgueiro Pardo. 2011. CST-News - a discourse-annotated corpus for single and multi-document summarization of news texts in Brazilian Portuguese. In *Proceedings of the 3rd RST Brazilian Meeting*, pages 88–105, Cuiabá, Brazil.

Lynn Carlson, Daniel Marcu, and Mary Ellen Okurovsky. 2001. Building a discourse-tagged corpus in the framework of Rhetorical Structure Theory. In *Proceedings of the Second SIGdial Workshop on Discourse and Dialogue*.

Yi Cheng and Sujian Li. 2019. Zero-shot Chinese discourse dependency parsing via cross-lingual mapping. In *Proceedings of the 1st Workshop on Discourse Structure in Neural NLG*, pages 24–29, Tokyo, Japan. Association for Computational Linguistics.

Alexis Conneau, Kartikay Khandelwal, Naman Goyal, Vishrav Chaudhary, Guillaume Wenzek, Francisco Guzmán, Edouard Grave, Myle Ott, Luke Zettlemoyer, and Veselin Stoyanov. 2020. Unsupervised cross-lingual representation learning at scale. In *Proceedings of the 58th Annual Meeting of the Association for Computational Linguistics*, pages 8440–8451, Online. Association for Computational Linguistics.

Iria da Cunha, Juan-Manuel Torres-Moreno, and Gerardo Sierra. 2011. On the development of the RST Spanish Treebank. In *Proceedings of the Fifth Linguistic Annotation Workshop (LAW V)*, pages 1–10, Portland, OR.

Jacob Devlin, Ming-Wei Chang, Kenton Lee, and Kristina Toutanova. 2019. BERT: Pre-training of deep bidirectional transformers for language understanding. In *Proceedings of the 2019 Conference of the North American Chapter of the Association for Computational Linguistics: Human Language Technologies, Volume 1 (Long and Short Papers)*, pages 4171–4186, Minneapolis, Minnesota. Association for Computational Linguistics.

Luke Gessler, Shabnam Behzad, Yang Janet Liu, Siyao Peng, Yilun Zhu, and Amir Zeldes. 2021. DisCoDisCo at the DISRPT2021 shared task: A system for discourse segmentation, classification, and connective detection. In *Proceedings of the 2nd Shared Task on Discourse Relation Parsing and Treebanking (DISRPT 2021)*, pages 51–62, Punta Cana, Dominican Republic. Association for Computational Linguistics.

Katsuhiko Hayashi, Tsutomu Hirao, and Masaaki Nagata. 2016. Empirical comparison of dependency conversions for RST discourse trees. In *Proceedings of the 17th Annual Meeting of the Special Interest Group on Discourse and Dialogue*, pages 128–136, Los Angeles. Association for Computational Linguistics.

Tsutomu Hirao, Yasuhisa Yoshida, Masaaki Nishino, Norihito Yasuda, and Masaaki Nagata. 2013. Single-document summarization as a tree knapsack problem. In *Proceedings of the 2013 Conference on Empirical Methods in Natural Language Processing*, pages 1515–1520, Seattle, Washington, USA. Association for Computational Linguistics.

Neil Houlsby, Andrei Giurgiu, Stanislaw Jastrzebski, Bruna Morrone, Quentin De Laroussilhe, Andrea Gesmundo, Mona Attariyan, and Sylvain Gelly. 2019.

Parameter-efficient transfer learning for NLP. In *International Conference on Machine Learning*, pages 2790–2799. PMLR.

Mikel Iruskieta, María Jesús Aranzabe, Arantza Diaz de Ilarraza, Itziar Gonzalez-Dios, Mikel Lersundi, and Oier Lopez de Lacalle. 2013. The RST Basque TreeBank: An online search interface to check rhetorical relations. In *4th Workshop on RST and Discourse Studies*, pages 40–49, Fortaleza, Brasil.

Anders Johannsen and Anders Søgaard. 2013. Disambiguating explicit discourse connectives without oracles. In *Proceedings of the Sixth International Joint Conference on Natural Language Processing*, pages 997–1001, Nagoya, Japan. Asian Federation of Natural Language Processing.

Olga Kovaleva, Alexey Romanov, Anna Rogers, and Anna Rumshisky. 2019. Revealing the dark secrets of BERT. In *Proceedings of the 2019 Conference on Empirical Methods in Natural Language Processing and the 9th International Joint Conference on Natural Language Processing (EMNLP-IJCNLP)*, pages 4365–4374, Hong Kong, China. Association for Computational Linguistics.

Zhengyuan Liu, Ke Shi, and Nancy Chen. 2020. Multilingual neural RST discourse parsing. In *Proceedings of the 28th International Conference on Computational Linguistics*, pages 6730–6738, Barcelona, Spain (Online). International Committee on Computational Linguistics.

Zhengyuan Liu, Ke Shi, and Nancy Chen. 2021. DMRST: A joint framework for document-level multilingual RST discourse segmentation and parsing. In *Proceedings of the 2nd Workshop on Computational Approaches to Discourse*, pages 154–164, Punta Cana, Dominican Republic and Online. Association for Computational Linguistics.

William C. Mann and Sandra A. Thompson. 1988. Rhetorical Structure Theory: Toward a functional theory of text organization. *Text*, 8:243–281.

Amália Mendes and Pierre Lejeune. 2022. Crpc-db a discourse bank for portuguese. In *Computational Processing of the Portuguese Language: 15th International Conference, PROPOR 2022, Fortaleza, Brazil, March 21–23, 2022, Proceedings*, page 79–89, Berlin, Heidelberg. Springer-Verlag.

Philippe Muller, Stergos Afantenos, Pascal Denis, and Nicholas Asher. 2012. Constrained decoding for text-level discourse parsing. In *Proceedings of COLING 2012*, pages 1883–1900, Mumbai, India. The COLING 2012 Organizing Committee.

Philippe Muller, Chloé Braud, and Mathieu Morey. 2019. ToNy: Contextual embeddings for accurate multilingual discourse segmentation of full documents. In *Proceedings of the Workshop on Discourse Relation Parsing and Treebanking 2019*, pages 115–124, Minneapolis, MN. Association for Computational Linguistics.

Minh Van Nguyen, Viet Dac Lai, Amir Pouran Ben Veyseh, and Thien Huu Nguyen. 2021. Trankit: A light-weight transformer-based toolkit for multilingual natural language processing. In *Proceedings of the 16th Conference of the European Chapter of the Association for Computational Linguistics: System Demonstrations*, pages 80–90, Online. Association for Computational Linguistics.

Noriki Nishida and Yuji Matsumoto. 2022. Out-of-domain discourse dependency parsing via bootstrapping: An empirical analysis on its effectiveness and limitation. *Transactions of the Association for Computational Linguistics*, 10:127–144.

Adam Paszke, Sam Gross, Francisco Massa, Adam Lerer, James Bradbury, Gregory Chanan, Trevor Killeen, Zeming Lin, Natalia Gimelshein, Luca Antiga, Alban Desmaison, Andreas Kopf, Edward Yang, Zachary DeVito, Martin Raison, Alykhan Tejani, Sasank Chilamkurthy, Benoit Steiner, Lu Fang, Junjie Bai, and Soumith Chintala. 2019. Pytorch: An imperative style, high-performance deep learning library. In *Advances in Neural Information Processing Systems 32*, pages 8024–8035. Curran Associates, Inc.

F. Pedregosa, G. Varoquaux, A. Gramfort, V. Michel, B. Thirion, O. Grisel, M. Blondel, P. Prettenhofer, R. Weiss, V. Dubourg, J. Vanderplas, A. Passos, D. Cournapeau, M. Brucher, M. Perrot, and E. Duchesnay. 2011. Scikit-learn: Machine learning in Python. *Journal of Machine Learning Research*, 12:2825–2830.

Jonas Pfeiffer, Andreas Rücklé, Clifton Poth, Aishwarya Kamath, Ivan Vulić, Sebastian Ruder, Kyunghyun Cho, and Iryna Gurevych. 2020. AdapterHub: A Framework for Adapting Transformers. In *Proceedings of the 2020 Conference on Empirical Methods in Natural Language Processing (EMNLP 2020): Systems Demonstrations*, pages 46–54, Online. Association for Computational Linguistics.

Jason Phang, Phil Yeres, Jesse Swanson, Haokun Liu, Ian F. Tenney, Phu Mon Htut, Clara Vania, Alex Wang, and Samuel R. Bowman. 2020. `jiant` 2.0: A software toolkit for research on general-purpose text understanding models. `http://jiant.info/`.

Emily Pitler, Mridhula Raghupathy, Hena Mehta, Ani Nenkova, Alan Lee, and Aravind Joshi. 2008. Easily identifiable discourse relations. In *Coling 2008: Companion volume: Posters*, pages 87–90, Manchester, UK. Coling 2008 Organizing Committee.

Rashmi Prasad, Aravind Joshi, Nikhil Dinesh, Alan Lee, Eleni Miltsakaki, and Bonnie Webber. 2005. The penn discourse treebank as a resource for natural language generation. In *Proceedings of the Corpus Linguistics Workshop on Using Corpora for Natural Language Generation*, pages 25–32.

Rashmi Prasad, Bonnie Webber, Alan Lee, and Aravind Joshi. 2019. Penn Discourse Treebank Version 3.0. LDC2019T05.

Gisela Redeker, Ildikó Berzlánovich, Nynke van der Vliet, Gosse Bouma, and Markus Egg. 2012. Multi-layer discourse annotation of a Dutch text corpus. In *Proceedings of LREC 2012*, pages 2820–2825, Istanbul, Turkey.

Giuseppe Riccardi, Evgeny A. Stepanov, and Shammur Absar Chowdhury. 2016. Discourse connective detection in spoken conversations. In *2016 IEEE International Conference on Acoustics, Speech and Signal Processing (ICASSP)*, pages 6095–6099.

Anna Rogers, Olga Kovaleva, and Anna Rumshisky. 2020. A primer in BERTology: What we know about how BERT works. *Transactions of the Association for Computational Linguistics*, 8:842–866.

Merel Scholman, Tianai Dong, Frances Yung, and Vera Demberg. 2021. Comparison of methods for explicit discourse connective identification across various domains. In *Proceedings of the 2nd Workshop on Computational Approaches to Discourse*, pages 95–106, Punta Cana, Dominican Republic and Online. Association for Computational Linguistics.

Sara Shahmohammadi, Hadi Veisi, and Ali Darzi. 2021. Persian Rhetorical Structure Theory. *arXiv preprint arXiv:2106.13833*.

Manfred Stede and Arne Neumann. 2014. Potsdam commentary corpus 2.0: Annotation for discourse research. In *Proceedings of the Ninth International Conference on Language Resources and Evaluation (LREC'14)*, pages 925–929, Reykjavik, Iceland. European Language Resources Association (ELRA).

Evgeny Stepanov and Giuseppe Riccardi. 2016. UniTN end-to-end discourse parser for CoNLL 2016 shared task. In *Proceedings of the CoNLL-16 shared task*, pages 85–91, Berlin, Germany. Association for Computational Linguistics.

Svetlana Toldova, Dina Pisarevskaya, Margarita Ananyeva, Maria Kobozeva, Alexander Nasedkin, Sofia Nikiforova, Irina Pavlova, and Alexey Shelepov. 2017. Rhetorical relations markers in Russian RST treebank. In *Proceedings of the 6th Workshop on Recent Advances in RST and Related Formalisms*, pages 29–33, Santiago de Compostela, Spain. Association for Computational Linguistics.

Sara Tonelli, Giuseppe Riccardi, Rashmi Prasad, and Aravind Joshi. 2010. Annotation of discourse relations for conversational spoken dialogs. In *Proceedings of the Seventh International Conference on Language Resources and Evaluation (LREC'10)*, Valletta, Malta. European Language Resources Association (ELRA).

Rachel Wicks and Matt Post. 2021. A unified approach to sentence segmentation of punctuated text in many languages. In *Proceedings of the 59th Annual Meeting of the Association for Computational Linguistics and the 11th International Joint Conference on Natural Language Processing (Volume 1: Long Papers)*, pages 3995–4007, Online. Association for Computational Linguistics.

Ngo Xuan Bach, Nguyen Le Minh, and Akira Shimazu. 2012. A reranking model for discourse segmentation using subtree features. In *Proceedings of the 13th Annual Meeting of the Special Interest Group on Discourse and Dialogue*, pages 160–168, Seoul, South Korea. Association for Computational Linguistics.

Nianwen Xue, Hwee Tou Ng, Sameer Pradhan, Attapol Rutherford, Bonnie Webber, Chuan Wang, and Hongmin Wang. 2016. CoNLL 2016 shared task on multilingual shallow discourse parsing. In *Proceedings of the CoNLL-16 shared task*, pages 1–19, Berlin, Germany. Association for Computational Linguistics.

An Yang and Sujian Li. 2018. SciDTB: Discourse dependency TreeBank for scientific abstracts. In *Proceedings of the 56th Annual Meeting of the Association for Computational Linguistics (Volume 2: Short Papers)*, pages 444–449, Melbourne, Australia. Association for Computational Linguistics.

Cheng Yi, Li Sujian, and Li Yueyuan. 2021. Unifying discourse resources with dependency framework. In *Proceedings of the 20th Chinese National Conference on Computational Linguistics*, pages 1058–1065, Huhhot, China. Chinese Information Processing Society of China.

Amir Zeldes. 2017. The GUM corpus: Creating multilayer resources in the classroom. *Language Resources and Evaluation*, 51(3):581–612.

Amir Zeldes, Debopam Das, Erick Galani Maziero, Juliano Antonio, and Mikel Iruskieta. 2019. The DISRPT 2019 shared task on elementary discourse unit segmentation and connective detection. In *Proceedings of the Workshop on Discourse Relation Parsing and Treebanking 2019*, pages 97–104, Minneapolis, MN. Association for Computational Linguistics.

Amir Zeldes, Yang Janet Liu, Mikel Iruskieta, Philippe Muller, Chloé Braud, and Sonia Badene. 2021. The DISRPT 2021 shared task on elementary discourse unit segmentation, connective detection, and relation classification. In *Proceedings of the 2nd Shared Task on Discourse Relation Parsing and Treebanking (DISRPT 2021)*, pages 1–12, Punta Cana, Dominican Republic. Association for Computational Linguistics.

Deniz Zeyrek and Murathan Kurfalı. 2017. TDB 1.1: Extensions on Turkish discourse bank. In *Proceedings of the 11th Linguistic Annotation Workshop*, pages 76–81, Valencia, Spain. Association for Computational Linguistics.

Deniz Zeyrek, Amália Mendes, Yulia Grishina, Murathan Kurfalı, Samuel Gibbon, and Maciej Ogrodniczuk. 2020. TED Multilingual Discourse Bank (TED-MDB): a parallel corpus annotated in the PDTB style. *Language Resources and Evaluation*, 54:587–613.

Deniz Zeyrek, Amália Mendes, and Murathan Kurfalı. 2018. Multilingual extension of PDTB-style annotation: The case of TED multilingual discourse bank. In *Proceedings of the Eleventh International Conference on Language Resources and Evaluation (LREC 2018)*, Miyazaki, Japan. European Language Resources Association (ELRA).

Deniz Zeyrek and Bonnie Webber. 2008. A discourse resource for Turkish: Annotating discourse connectives in the METU corpus. In *Proceedings of the 6th Workshop on Asian Language Resources*.

Yuping Zhou, Jill Lu, Jennifer Zhang, and Nianwen Xue. 2014. Chinese discourse treebank 0.5 ldc2014t21. *Web Download. Philadelphia: Linguistic Data Consortium*.

Corpus	Treebanked			Plain		
	F1 dev	F1 test	DD21	F1 dev	F1 test	DD21
			Segmentation			
deu.rst.pcc	96.79	**97.30**	95.58	96.60	**96.60**	93.94
eng.rst.gum	95.54	**95.55**	94.15	95.78	**94.97**	92.61
eng.rst.rstdt	97.33	**97.11**	96.64	97.60	**97.45**	96.35
eus.rst.ert	91.69	**91.56**	90.46	91.83	**92.38**	90.47
fas.rst.prstc	93.79	**93.88**	92.94	94.05	92.56	**92.86**
nld.rst.nldt	97.51	**97.47**	95.97	97.09	**97.63**	94.69
por.rst.cstn	94.06	93.48	**94.35**	93.50	94.08	**94.11**
rus.rst.rrt	86.80	85.86	**86.21**	84.75	85.46	**85.74**
spa.rst.rststb	96.19	**92.67**	92.22	96.32	**92.31**	91.76
spa.rst.sctb	86.88	**84.40**	82.48	85.44	**87.16**	80.86
zho.rst.gcdt	92.69	92.30	-	92.20	91.78	-
zho.rst.sctb	79.05	81.18	**83.34**	77.53	75.29	**76.21**
eng.sdrt.stac	94.77	94.83	**94.91**	91.57	90.69	**91.91**
fra.sdrt.annodis	90.27	89.54	**90.02**	90.17	**91.40**	85.78
∗**eng.dep.covdtb**	91.32	91.41	-	91.65	92.26	-
eng.dep.scidtb	96.18	95.44	-	95.63	94.89	-
zho.dep.scidtb	93.33	90.40	-	93.01	89.64	-
Mean	92.60	92.02	-	92.04	91.56	-
Mean corpora 2021	-	**91.91**	91.48	-	**91.38**	89.79
			Connective identification			
eng.pdtb.pdtb	94.41	**92.38**	92.02	93.94	92.25	**92.56**
∗**eng.pdtb.tedm**	75.86	77.88	-	80.00	80.63	-
ita.pdtb.luna	79.72	64.08	-	74.19	70.17	-
por.pdtb.crpc	85.16	81.74	-	84.65	80.26	-
∗**por.pdtb.tedm**	73.08	75.23	-	71.22	77.60	-
∗**tha.pdtb.tdtb**	87.43	86.42	-	74.32	69.32	-
tur.pdtb.tdb	89.73	92.48	**94.11**	89.69	**93.57**	93.56
∗**tur.pdtb.tedm**	65.42	66.33	-	64.15	64.27	-
zho.pdtb.cdtb	87.66	**89.95**	87.52	87.77	**90.43**	88.35
Average	82.05	80.72	-	79.99	79.83	-
Mean corpora 2021	-	**92.30**	91.22	-	**91.78**	91.49

Table 8: DisCut: Results (F1) on the dev and test sets for segmentation and discourse connective identification. Models with RoBERTa-large, freezing layers 0-5. 'DD21' stands for DiscoDisco 2021, the system ranked first in DISRPT 2021. 'Mean corpora 2021' is the mean F1 without considering the corpora added in DISRPT 2023.

A Additional results

The table 8 corresponds to the scores we obtain on the test sets, that can be compared to the ones obtained by the organizers when reproducing our system, as given in Table 2.

HITS at DISRPT 2023: Discourse Segmentation, Connective Detection, and Relation Classification

Wei Liu* and **Fan Yi*** and **Michael Strube**
Heidelberg Institute for Theoretical Studies
{wei.liu, yi.fan, michael.strube}@h-its.org

Abstract

HITS participated in the Discourse Segmentation (DS, Task 1) and Connective Detection (CD, Task 2) tasks at the DISRPT 2023. Task 1 focuses on segmenting the text into discourse units, while Task 2 aims to detect the discourse connectives. We deployed a framework based on different pre-trained models according to the target language for these two tasks.

HITS also participated in the Relation Classification track (Task 3). The main task was recognizing the discourse relation between text spans from different languages. We designed a joint model for languages with a small corpus while separate models for large corpora. The adversarial training strategy is applied to enhance the robustness of relation classifiers.

The implementation of our models for three tasks is available at https://github.com/liuwei1206/disrpt2023.

1 Task and Data

The 2023 shared task provides 3 sub-tasks, including discourse segmentation (DS, Task 1), Connective Detection (CD, Task 2), and Relation Classification (RC, Task 3).

Task 1 focuses on conducting discourse units segmentation under different formalisms, such as Rhetorical Structure Theory (RST, MANN and Thompson, 1988), Segmented Discourse Representation Theory (SDRT, Lascarides and Asher, 2007) and Penn Discourse Treebank (PDTB, Miltsakaki et al., 2004). As different corpora, languages and formalisms or theories use different segmentation guidelines, the challenge is to design flexible methods to deal with various situations. The aim of Task 2 is to identify discourse connectives in the text.

Relation classification aims to identify the discourse relation, such as *Cause* and *Comparison*, between two text spans. The shared task provides 26 corpora covering 13 languages, including Basque, Chinese, Dutch, English, French, German, Italian, Persia, Portugal, Russian, Spanish, Thai, and Turkish. Most of corpora are annotated with Rhetorical Structure Theory (RST, MANN and Thompson, 1988) and Penn Discourse Treebank (PDTB, Miltsakaki et al., 2004), with a small part using Segmented Discourse Representation Theory (SDRT, Lascarides and Asher, 2007) and Discourse Dependency Framework (DEP, Stede et al., 2016). We show the statistics of relation corpora in Table 2.

*Equal contribution. Wei is responsible for relation classification, while Yi works on discourse segmentation and connective detection.

2 Discourse Segmentation and Connective Detection

2.1 Approach

Our framework for Task 1 and Task 2 is composed of a BERT-based model (Devlin et al., 2019), Bi-LSTM (Hochreiter and Schmidhuber, 1997) and conditional random field (CRF, Lafferty et al., 2001). In our framework, we first obtain the embedding of the input text via a BERT-based model. We then use Bi-LSTM to capture the contextual information and generate a richer contextual representation by exploiting the sequential relationships between words. Finally, CRF can globally optimise the label sequence based on the contextual information of the current word and the relationship between the preceding and following labels, resulting in better consistency and rationality of the predicted label sequence.

2.2 Experiments

As the BERT-based model provides the embedding for the input text, choosing an appropriate one according to the language is essential for the framework. We choose at least two pre-trained BERT-based models for each language and fine-tune the parameters to achieve the best performance for our framework. After several experiments and comparing different BERT-based models, our final choice for the BERT-based model for different languages

Proceedings of the 3rd Shared Task on Discourse Relation Parsing and Treebanking (DISRPT 2023), pages 43–49
July 14, 2023 ©2023 Association for Computational Linguistics

Framework	Corpus	Task 1/2				Task3			
		Label	Train	Dev	Test	Label	Train	Dev	Test
RST	deu.rst.pcc (Stede and Neumann, 2014)	2	1773	207	213	26	2164	241	260
	eng.rst.gum (Zeldes, 2017)	2	9234	1221	1201	14	19497	2618	2576
	eng.rst.rstdt (Lynn Carlson, 2002; Carlson et al., 2003)	2	6672	717	929	17	16003	1622	2156
	eus.rst.ert (Iruskieta et al., 2013; Aranzabe et al., 2015)	2	1599	366	415	29	2534	679	615
	fas.rst.prstc (Shahmohammadi et al., 2021)	2	1713	202	264	17	4101	500	593
	nld.rst.nldt (Redeker et al., 2012)	2	1156	255	240	32	1609	332	326
	por.rst.cstn (Cardoso et al., 2011)	2	1825	257	139	32	8798	1286	1249
	rus.rst.rrt (Pisarevskaya et al., 2017; Toldova et al., 2017)	2	18932	2025	2087	22	28869	2856	2844
	spa.rst.rststb (da Cunha et al., 2011)	2	1548	254	287	28	2241	384	427
	spa.rst.sctb (Cao et al., 2018a, 2017b,a, 2016)	2	326	76	114	24	440	95	160
	zho.rst.sctb (Cao et al., 2018b, 2017c,a, 2016)	2	361	86	133	26	440	95	160
	zho.rst.gcdt (Peng et al., 2022)	2	2026	331	335	31	6455	1007	954
PDTB	eng.pdtb.pdtb (Webber et al., 2019)	3	44563	1703	2364	23	43920	1674	2257
	eng.pdtb.tedm (Zeyrek et al., 2018)	3	-	143	238	20	-	179	352
	ita.pdtb.luna (Tonelli et al., 2010)	2	3721	775	1315	15	957	211	382
	por.pdtb.crpc (Mendes and Lejeune, 2022)	3	4078	581	535	22	8798	1286	1249
	por.pdtb.tedm (Zeyrek et al., 2018)	3	-	148	246	20	-	191	365
	tha.pdtb.tdtb	3	5076	633	825	20	8279	1244	1345
	tur.pdtb.tdb (Zeyrek Bozşahin et al., 2013)	3	24960	2948	3289	23	2452	313	423
	tur.pdtb.tedm (Zeyrek et al., 2018)	3	-	141	269	23	-	214	365
	zho.pdtb.cdtb (Zhou et al., 2014)	3	2049	438	404	9	3657	855	758
SDRT	eng.sdrt.stac (Asher et al., 2016)	2	8754	991	1342	16	9581	1146	1511
	fra.sdrt.annodis (Afantenos et al., 2012)	2	1020	245	242	18	2186	529	626
DEP	eng.dep.covdtb (Nishida and Matsumoto, 2022)	2	-	1162	1181	12	-	2400	2587
	eng.dep.scidtb (Yang and Li, 2018)	2	2570	815	817	24	6061	1934	1912
	zho.dep.scidtb (Cheng and Li, 2019)	2	308	103	89	23	803	282	216

Table 1: Statistics of corpora provided by the shared task.

Language	Pre-trained model choice
deu	xlm-roberta-base
eng	roberta-base
eus	ixa-ehu/berteus-base-cased
fas	HooshvareLab/bert-fa-base-uncased
fra	xlm-roberta-base
ita	xlm-roberta-base
nld	pdelobelle/robbert-v2-dutch-base
por	neuralmind/bert-base-portuguese-cased
rus	DeepPavlov/rubert-base-cased
spa	dccuchile/bert-base-spanish-wwm-cased
tur	dbmdz/bert-base-turkish-cased
zho	bert-base-chinese
tha	airesearch/wangchanberta-base-att-spm-uncased

Table 2: Model choice for different languages

is shown in Table 2. Our framework is trained with batch size 16 for each corpus, and the maximum input sequence length is 512. If the input sequence length exceeds 512, then our framework will slice it into two or more segments. The maximum length of all segments is also 512. The LSTM in our framework has two layers, and both of them are bi-directional. The criterion that we choose those BERT-based models in our framework is their best performance with corresponding parameters. In addition, all the pre-trained models we use for this shared task are provided by HuggingFace[*]. The result of our framework's performance with golden treebanked data for Task 1 and Task 2 shows in Table 3. We use our trained model on another corpus to evaluate corpora that do not have a training corpus and select the best one, shown in Table 4.

However, due to the time limitation, we only tuned all pre-trained models and tested our framework with the golden treebanked data as the input. Besides, we observed that normally the larger model performs better than the base model. For instance, for the corpus eng.dep.scidtb, we use the best parameters we tuned for the Roberta-base model (Liu et al., 2019) for the Roberta-large model, our framework's performance will increase 0.28% and 0.11% in the development set and test set separately. Also, we tried the Adversarial Training strategy (Miyato et al., 2016) and the Bootstrap aggregating strategy (Breiman, 1996), which is a commonly used ensemble learning method, separately with our framework. We only test the Bootstrap aggregating strategy on the corpus ita.pdtb.luna. We use the best and second-best learning rates on training with our framework to generate two models first. Then, we change the xlm-base model to dbmdz/bert-base-italian-uncased, and also apply the best and second-best learning rates to generate two trained models. Every time when we train these models, we tune the

[*] https://huggingface.co/

Corpus	F_1
deu.rst.pcc	96.19%
eng.rst.gum	81.22%
eng.rst.rstdt	97.36%
eus.rst.ert	89.85%
fas.rst.prstc	93.05%
nld.rst.nldt	93.64%
por.rst.cstn	94.63%
rus.rst.rrt	85.05%
spa.rst.rststb	90.87%
spa.rst.sctb	83.17%
zho.rst.sctb	80.12%
zho.rst.gcdt	91.37%
eng.pdtb.pdtb	93.47%
ita.pdtb.luna	66.41%
por.pdtb.crpc	79.74%
tha.pdtb.tdtb	86.92%
tur.pdtb.tdb	84.89%
zho.pdtb.cdtb	87.40%
eng.sdrt.stac	95.84%
fra.sdrt.annodis	88.45%
eng.dep.scidtb	94.97%
zho.dep.scidtb	90.59%
Mean	88.41%

Table 3: Results of Task 1 and Task 2 for corpora with a training dataset

ratio of the corpus to 1 means we use the whole corpus. Note that we can tune the ratio to sample randomly the percentage of data from the training dataset. Then we let all models vote in the development set and test set. Finally, we tally the results of the voting to determine the final model predictions. In our experiment setting, we follow the majority vote, which implies every vote contributes equally to the final result and the most voted result is selected. We found this simple setting of Bootstrap aggregating strategy can improve the F1 score by 0.16% and 0.13% on the development set and test set respectively. During the test of the Adversarial Training strategy, we only test on a few corpora. The result shows in Table 5. We observe that the performance increases in almost all corpora we test, which means this strategy functions. Insufficient time prevented us from exploring the result for the Adversarial Training strategy, the Bootstrap aggregating strategy, and the larger pre-trained models separately and in combinations of them on all corpora with plain text input and golden treebanked input settings.

Corpus	F_1	model source
eng.pdtb.tedm	78.56%	eng.pdtb.pdtb
por.pdtb.tedm	80.19%	por.pdtb.crpc
tur.pdtb.tedm	66.15%	tur.pdtb.tdb
eng.dep.covdtb	90.14%	eng.dep.scidtb
Mean	78.76%	-

Table 4: Results of Task 1 and Task 2 for corpora without a training dataset. The models used for generating the result are trained on is noted in the model source column.

Corpus	F_1	vs. without adv
deu.rst.pcc	96.59%	+0.40%
eng.sdrt.stac	97.21%	−0.15%
eus.rst.ert	90.10%	+0.25%
fas.rst.prstc	93.14%	+0.09%
nld.rst.nldt	96.46%	+2.82%
por.rst.cstn	95.85%	+1.22%
spa.rst.rststb	91.02%	+0.15%
spa.rst.sctb	83.76%	+0.59%
Mean	93.02%	+0.67125%

Table 5: Comparison between applying Adversarial Training strategy and without it for our framework on the dataset we have tested.

3 Relation Classification

3.1 Approach

The relation classifiers employed in this work follow an architecture widely used for text classification tasks: pre-trained models as the encoder and a linear network as the classification layer. The training of classifiers on each corpus varies from each other depending on the corpus size. Specifically, we train individual classifiers for large corpora (e.g., eng.pdtb.pdtb) but a joint model for a set of small datasets. This is because a large number of instances is sufficient to train a good classifier, while a small corpus can lead to underfitting.

For large corpora, including eng.rst.gum, eng.rst.rstdt, eus.rst.ert, zho.rst.gcdt, eng.pdtb.pdtb, eng.sdrt.stac, and fra.sdrt.annodis, individual classifiers are trained for them. For small corpora, we divide them into three groups according their annotation framework. The first is the **RST-group**, containing deu.rst.pcc, fas.rst.prstc, nld.rst.nldt, por.rst.cstn, rus.rst.rrt, spa.rst.rststb, spa.rst.sctb, and zho.rst.sctb. We train a joint model called **joint-RST** on the RST-group corpus. The second is the **PDTB-group**, covering ita.pdtb.luna,

Model type	Corpus	Encoder
individual	eng.rst.gum	roberta-large
	eng.rst.rstdt	
	eng.pdtb.pdtb	
	eng.sdrt.stac	
	eus.rst.ert	berteus-base-cased
	zho.rst.gcdt	macbert-large
	zho.pdtb.cdtb	
	fra.sdrt.annodis	camembert-large
joint-RST	deu.rst.pcc	xlm-roberta-large
	fas.rst.prstc	
	nld.rst.nldt	
	por.rst.cstn	
	rus.rst.rrt	
	spa.rst.rststb	
	spa.rst.sctb	
	zho.rst.sctb	
joint-PDTB	eng.pdtb.tedm	
	ita.pdtb.luna	
	por.pdtb.crpc	
	por.pdtb.tedm	
	tha.pdtb.tdtb	
	tur.pdtb.tdb	
	tur.pdtb.tedm	
joint-DEP	eng.dep.scidtb	
	eng.dep.covdtb	
	zho.dep.scidtb	

Table 6: Training strategy for different relation corpora. "individual" means training a corpus-specific model.

Model type	Corpus	Accuracy
Individual	eng.rst.gum	65.67
	eng.rst.rstdt	66.40
	eng.pdtb.pdtb	74.75
	eng.sdrt.stac	62.85
	eus.rst.ert	56.64
	zho.rst.gcdt	56.14
	zho.pdtb.pdtb	85.36
	fra.sdrt.annodis	50.08
joint-RST	deu.rst.pcc	35.77
	fas.rst.prstc	55.91
	nld.rst.nldt	55.69
	por.rst.cstn	68.38
	rus.rst.rrt	62.05
	spa.rst.rststb	58.69
	spa.pdtb.crpc	64.15
	zho.rst.sctb	62.26
joint-PDTB	ita.pdtb.luna	67.89
	por.pdtb.crpc	77.80
	tha.pdtb.tdtb	96.80
	tur.pdtb.tdb	56.64
joint-DEP	eng.dep.scidtb	75.30
	zho.dep.scidtb	67.44
	Mean	64.67

Table 7: Results (Task 3) for corpora with a training set.

Corpus	Accuracy
eng.pdtb.tedm	65.53
por.pdtb.tedm	67.03
tur.pdtb.tedm	56.87
eng.dep.covdtb	70.03
Mean	64.87

Table 8: Results (Task 3) for corpora without a training set.

por.pdtb.crpc, tha.pdtb.tdtb, and tur.pdtb.tdb, and the joint model **joint-PDTB** is trained on this group. The last is the **DEP-group**, including eng.dep.scidtb and zho.dep.scidtb, and its corresponding model is **joint-DEP**.

During training, adversarial strategy (Miyato et al., 2016) is applied to improve the robustness of classifiers. For corpora without a training set, we evaluate them with the joint model of the corresponding annotation framework. We summarize the setup for each corpus in Table 6.

3.2 Experiments

We train relation classifiers based on the corpora provided by the shared task. During the evaluation, we report the result of a model on the test set using the checkpoint that achieves the best performance on the development set.

Table 7 shows the results on corpora with training sets. We find that small corpora can significantly benefit from joint training. For example, the joint-RST outperforms a relation classifier trained on deu.rst.pcc solely more than 5 points (i.e., 30.00% $\rightarrow$ 35.77%). However, the joint model performs worse on large corpora, such as eng.rst.gum, decreasing the accuracy from 65.67% to 62.06%, compared to the individual model. Due to time constraints, we can not finish the ablation study on all corpora.

The shared task also provides evaluation corpora without training sets. The primary goal is to test the zero-shot performance of trained classifiers. Our joint models are well suited for this setting since they have a large label set, inheriting from a group of small corpora. Table 8 shows joint models' results on those evaluation corpora. Surprisingly, our joint models perform well under the zero-shot setting, achieving an average accuracy of 64.87%, close to the performance of corpora with a training set (i.e., 64.67%).

4 Conclusion

In this paper, we present our models in the shared task DISRPT 2023. For Tasks 1 and 2, we employ a pre-trained model+BiLSTM+CRF to capture textual information and dependency between successive labels. For Task 3, we design a joint training strategy for small corpora, which can compensate for underfitting caused by limited training instances.

Acknowledgements

The authors would like to thank the anonymous reviewers for their comments. This work has been funded by the Klaus Tschira Foundation, Heidelberg, Germany.

References

Stergos Afantenos, Nicholas Asher, Farah Benamara, Myriam Bras, Cécile Fabre, Mai Ho-dac, Anne Le Draoulec, Philippe Muller, Marie-Paule Péry-Woodley, Laurent Prévot, Josette Rebeyrolles, Ludovic Tanguy, Marianne Vergez-Couret, and Laure Vieu. 2012. An empirical resource for discovering cognitive principles of discourse organisation: the ANNODIS corpus. In *Proceedings of the Eighth International Conference on Language Resources and Evaluation (LREC'12)*, pages 2727–2734, Istanbul, Turkey. European Language Resources Association (ELRA).

María Jesús Aranzabe, Aitziber Atutxa, Kepa Bengoetxea, Arantza Díaz, Deliana Ilarraza, Iakes Goenaga, and Koldo Gojenola. 2015. Automatic conversion of the basque dependency treebank to universal dependencies. In *the fourteenth international workshop on treebanks an linguistic theories (TLT14)*, pages 233–241, Warsaw, Poland.

Nicholas Asher, Julie Hunter, Mathieu Morey, Benamara Farah, and Stergos Afantenos. 2016. Discourse structure and dialogue acts in multiparty dialogue: the STAC corpus. In *Proceedings of the Tenth International Conference on Language Resources and Evaluation (LREC'16)*, pages 2721–2727, Portorož, Slovenia. European Language Resources Association (ELRA).

Leo Breiman. 1996. Bagging predictors. *Machine Learning*, 24(2):123–140.

Shuyuan Cao, Iria da Cunha, and Mikel Iruskieta. 2016. A corpus-based approach for Spanish-Chinese language learning. In *Proceedings of the 3rd Workshop on Natural Language Processing Techniques for Educational Applications (NLPTEA2016)*, pages 97–106, Osaka, Japan. The COLING 2016 Organizing Committee.

Shuyuan Cao, Iria Da-Cunha, and Mikel Iruskieta. 2017a. Toward the elaboration of a spanish-chinese parallel annotated corpus. In *Professional and Academic Discourse: an Interdisciplinary Perspective*, volume 2 of *EPiC Series in Language and Linguistics*, pages 315–324. EasyChair.

Shuyuan Cao, Iria da Cunha, and Mikel Iruskieta. 2018a. The RST Spanish-Chinese treebank. In *Proceedings of the Joint Workshop on Linguistic Annotation, Multiword Expressions and Constructions (LAW-MWE-CxG-2018)*, pages 156–166, Santa Fe, New Mexico, USA. Association for Computational Linguistics.

Shuyuan Cao, Iria da Cunha, and Mikel Iruskieta. 2018b. The RST Spanish-Chinese treebank. In *Proceedings of the Joint Workshop on Linguistic Annotation, Multiword Expressions and Constructions (LAW-MWE-CxG-2018)*, pages 156–166, Santa Fe, New Mexico, USA. Association for Computational Linguistics.

Shuyuan Cao, Nianwen Xue, Iria da Cunha, Mikel Iruskieta, and Chuan Wang. 2017b. Discourse segmentation for building a RST Chinese treebank. In *Proceedings of the 6th Workshop on Recent Advances in RST and Related Formalisms*, pages 73–81, Santiago de Compostela, Spain. Association for Computational Linguistics.

Shuyuan Cao, Nianwen Xue, Iria da Cunha, Mikel Iruskieta, and Chuan Wang. 2017c. Discourse segmentation for building a RST Chinese treebank. In *Proceedings of the 6th Workshop on Recent Advances in RST and Related Formalisms*, pages 73–81, Santiago de Compostela, Spain. Association for Computational Linguistics.

Paula Christina Figueira Cardoso, Erick Galani Maziero, Maria Lucía del Rosario Castro Jorge, M. Eloize, R. Kibar Aji Seno, Ariani Di Felippo, Lucia Helena Machado Rino, Maria das Graças Volpe Nunes, and Thiago Alexandre Salgueiro Pardo. 2011. CST-News - a discourse-annotated corpus for single and multi-document summarization of news texts in Brazilian Portuguese. In *Proceedings of the 3rd RST Brazilian Meeting*, pages 88–105, Cuiabá, Brazil.

Lynn Carlson, Daniel Marcu, and Mary Ellen Okurowski. 2003. Building a Discourse-Tagged Corpus in the Framework of Rhetorical Structure Theory. In *Current and New Directions in Discourse and Dialogue*, Text, Speech and Language Technology 22, pages 85–112. Kluwer, Dordrecht.

Yi Cheng and Sujian Li. 2019. Zero-shot Chinese discourse dependency parsing via cross-lingual mapping. In *Proceedings of the 1st Workshop on Discourse Structure in Neural NLG*, pages 24–29, Tokyo, Japan. Association for Computational Linguistics.

Iria da Cunha, Juan-Manuel Torres-Moreno, and Gerardo Sierra. 2011. On the development of the RST Spanish treebank. In *Proceedings of the 5th Linguistic Annotation Workshop*, pages 1–10, Portland, Oregon, USA. Association for Computational Linguistics.

Jacob Devlin, Ming-Wei Chang, Kenton Lee, and Kristina Toutanova. 2019. BERT: Pre-training of deep bidirectional transformers for language understanding. In *Proceedings of the 2019 Conference of the North American Chapter of the Association for Computational Linguistics: Human Language Technologies, Volume 1 (Long and Short Papers)*, pages 4171–4186, Minneapolis, Minnesota. Association for Computational Linguistics.

Sepp Hochreiter and Jürgen Schmidhuber. 1997. Long short-term memory. *Neural Comput.*, 9(8):1735–1780.

Mikel Iruskieta, María Jesús Aranzabe, Arantza Diaz de Ilarraza, Itziar Gonzalez-Dios, Mikel Lersundi, and Oier Lopez de Lacalle. 2013. The RST Basque TreeBank: An online search interface to check rhetorical relations. In *4th Workshop on RST and Discourse Studies*, pages 40–49, Fortaleza, Brasil.

John D. Lafferty, Andrew McCallum, and Fernando C. N. Pereira. 2001. Conditional random fields: Probabilistic models for segmenting and labeling sequence data. In *Proceedings of the Eighteenth International Conference on Machine Learning*, ICML '01, page 282–289, San Francisco, CA, USA. Morgan Kaufmann Publishers Inc.

Alex Lascarides and Nicholas Asher. 2007. *Segmented Discourse Representation Theory: Dynamic Semantics With Discourse Structure*, volume 3, pages 87–124.

Yinhan Liu, Myle Ott, Naman Goyal, Jingfei Du, Mandar Joshi, Danqi Chen, Omer Levy, Mike Lewis, Luke Zettlemoyer, and Veselin Stoyanov. 2019. Roberta: A robustly optimized BERT pretraining approach. *CoRR*, abs/1907.11692.

Mary Ellen Okurowski Lynn Carlson, Daniel Marcu. 2002. RST Discourse Treebank LDC2002T07.

WILLIAM MANN and Sandra Thompson. 1988. Rethorical structure theory: Toward a functional theory of text organization. *Text*, 8:243–281.

Amália Mendes and Pierre Lejeune. 2022. Crpc-db a discourse bank for portuguese. In *Computational Processing of the Portuguese Language: 15th International Conference, PROPOR 2022, Fortaleza, Brazil, March 21–23, 2022, Proceedings*, pages 79–89. Springer.

Eleni Miltsakaki, Rashmi Prasad, Aravind Joshi, and Bonnie Webber. 2004. The Penn Discourse Treebank. In *Proceedings of the Fourth International Conference on Language Resources and Evaluation (LREC'04)*, Lisbon, Portugal. European Language Resources Association (ELRA).

Takeru Miyato, Andrew M Dai, and Ian Goodfellow. 2016. Adversarial training methods for semi-supervised text classification. *arXiv preprint arXiv:1605.07725*.

Noriki Nishida and Yuji Matsumoto. 2022. Out-of-domain discourse dependency parsing via bootstrapping: An empirical analysis on its effectiveness and limitation. *Transactions of the Association for Computational Linguistics*, 10:127–144.

Siyao Peng, Yang Janet Liu, and Amir Zeldes. 2022. Chinese Discourse Annotation Reference Manual. Research Report, Georgetown University (Washington, D.C.).

Dina Pisarevskaya, Margarita Ananyeva, Maria Kobozeva, A. Nasedkin, S. Nikiforova, I. Pavlova, and A. Shelepov. 2017. Towards building a discourse-annotated corpus of russian. In *Computational Linguistics and Intellectual Technologies: 23rd International Conference on Computational Linguistics and Intellectual Technologies "Dialogue"*, pages 194–204.

Gisela Redeker, Ildikó Berzlánovich, Nynke van der Vliet, Gosse Bouma, and Markus Egg. 2012. Multi-layer discourse annotation of a Dutch text corpus. In *Proceedings of the Eighth International Conference on Language Resources and Evaluation (LREC'12)*, pages 2820–2825, Istanbul, Turkey. European Language Resources Association (ELRA).

Sara Shahmohammadi, Hadi Veisi, and Ali Darzi. 2021. Persian Rhetorical Structure Theory. *arXiv preprint arXiv:2106.13833*.

Manfred Stede, Stergos Afantenos, Andreas Peldszus, Nicholas Asher, and Jérémy Perret. 2016. Parallel discourse annotations on a corpus of short texts. In *Proceedings of the Tenth International Conference on Language Resources and Evaluation (LREC'16)*, pages 1051–1058, Portorož, Slovenia. European Language Resources Association (ELRA).

Manfred Stede and Arne Neumann. 2014. Potsdam commentary corpus 2.0: Annotation for discourse research. In *Proceedings of the Ninth International Conference on Language Resources and Evaluation (LREC'14)*, pages 925–929, Reykjavik, Iceland. European Language Resources Association (ELRA).

Svetlana Toldova, Dina Pisarevskaya, Margarita Ananyeva, Maria Kobozeva, Alexander Nasedkin, Sofia Nikiforova, Irina Pavlova, and Alexey Shelepov. 2017. Rhetorical relations markers in Russian RST treebank. In *Proceedings of the 6th Workshop on Recent Advances in RST and Related Formalisms*, pages 29–33, Santiago de Compostela, Spain. Association for Computational Linguistics.

Sara Tonelli, Giuseppe Riccardi, Rashmi Prasad, and Aravind Joshi. 2010. Annotation of discourse relations for conversational spoken dialogs. In *Proceedings of the Seventh International Conference on Language Resources and Evaluation (LREC'10)*, Valletta, Malta. European Language Resources Association (ELRA).

Bonnie Webber, Rashmi Prasad, Alan Lee, and Aravind Joshi. 2019. The penn discourse treebank 3.0 annotation manual. *Philadelphia, University of Pennsylvania*, 35:108.

An Yang and Sujian Li. 2018. SciDTB: Discourse dependency TreeBank for scientific abstracts. In *Proceedings of the 56th Annual Meeting of the Association for Computational Linguistics (Volume 2: Short Papers)*, pages 444–449, Melbourne, Australia. Association for Computational Linguistics.

Amir Zeldes. 2017. The GUM Corpus: Creating multilayer resources in the classroom. *Language Resources and Evaluation*, 51(3):581–612.

Deniz Zeyrek, Amália Mendes, and Murathan Kurfalı. 2018. Multilingual extension of PDTB-style annotation: The case of TED multilingual discourse bank. In *Proceedings of the Eleventh International Conference on Language Resources and Evaluation (LREC 2018)*, Miyazaki, Japan. European Language Resources Association (ELRA).

Deniz Zeyrek Bozşahin, Ayışığı B. Sevdik Çallı, and Ruket Çakıcı. 2013. Turkish discourse bank: Porting a discourse annotation style to a morphologically rich language. *Dialogue and Discourse*, page 174–184.

Yuping Zhou, Jill Lu, Jennifer Zhang, and Nianwen Xue. 2014. Chinese discourse treebank 0.5. *LDC*.

Author Index

Association for Computational Linguistics
209 N. Eighth Street
Stroudsburg, Pennsylvania 18360

ISBN 978-1-7138-8181-0

CURRAN ASSOCIATES INC.
proceedings.com

2nd Conference of the Asia-Pacific Chapter of the Association for Computational Linguistics and the 12th International Joint Conference on Natural Language Processing (AACL-IJCNLP 2022)

Tutorial Abstracts

Online
20-21 November 2022